CHURCHES OF NORFOLK

JOHN E. VIGAR

AMBERLEY

This edition first published 2021

Amberley Publishing
The Hill, Stroud
Gloucestershire GL5 4EP

www.amberley-books.com

British Library Cataloguing in Publication Data.
A catalogue record for this book is available from the British Library.

ISBN 978 1 3981 0626 0 (print)
ISBN 978 1 3981 0627 7 (ebook)

Typesetting by SJmagic DESIGN SERVICES, India.
Printed in Great Britain.

Contents

Introduction

Nobody knows how many Anglican churches there are in Norfolk. By 1254, when the first official list was compiled, there were 818 and best guesses today are that there are over a thousand. Included in this figure are all the active churches, seventy conserved redundant churches, 160 ruins and remains of dozens of monastic churches that didn't survive the Reformation. There are more medieval churches in Norfolk per head of population than anywhere else in Europe. No wonder people come to the county just to visit churches and the Diocese of Norwich and, to a lesser extent, the Diocese of Ely in whose remits the churches fall actively encourage tourism. As a result nearly 80 per cent of Norfolk churches are open every day – and even more in summer. Why there should be so many churches is an accident of history, deriving from early settlement, foreign incursions, monastic foundation, pilgrimage, trade and personal wealth.

The development of Norfolk churches is like those in the rest of East Anglia. The vast majority were founded in the Saxon or early Norman period. In the thirteenth century they were usually rebuilt and extended to suit changes in liturgical practice. This always included the extension of or rebuilding of the chancel and sometimes the addition of an aisle. Following the Black Death (1348) there was a spurt of investment in buildings which often included the installation of new windows, fonts and porches. The last period of structural change occurred between around 1450 and 1530 and is the one period for which Norfolk churches are best known. By this time the county had a population of over 100,000, which represented one of the densest populations in the England. Yet if you disregard 25,000 as the population of Norwich, that figure of seventy-five people per rural church is extremely high and shows that the vastness of many Norfolk churches has more to do with personal wealth than size of population alone.

How do Norfolk churches differ from other counties? Firstly, where money was available, they can be huge as donors, perhaps feeling guilty of their wealth, beautified them in order to save their souls in the afterlife. Towers are a feature of the county, particularly noticeable in the number of much-loved round towers. There are 131 of these in Norfolk out of a total of 180 countrywide and they are purely a local fashion, probably introduced from Scandinavia. Despite local hearsay, the vast majority are Norman or later in date, and many had new tops added in subsequent periods. The more usual square towers have their own local characteristic as well in the form of a window opening halfway up the tower. These are known as sound holes and seem to have been to light and ventilate the ringing floor. Like everything in our churches, they are as plain or fancy as money allowed. Inside our churches three items of furnishing stand out. Firstly fonts, where a distinct type, the Seven Sacrament font, reigns supreme. These octagonal fonts have seven of their side panels carved with depictions of the sacraments. There are twenty-five in Norfolk out of forty countrywide. Secondly, Norfolk is known for its rood screens. Although these were usually destroyed during the Reformation, Norfolk has over 200 surviving, at least in part. Many of these retain substantial traces of their original painted decoration. Thirdly we should look at the church roof. Whilst these take many different forms, Norfolk has over forty churches with elaborate roof structures that display carved angel decorations, either as flat images against the roof, or three-dimensional figures standing upright. Again, this is the largest concentration of such roofs in the country.

In a small book choosing just fifty churches to represent the county has not been easy. I want to show you churches that reflect different periods, styles and locations and especially want to introduce many that are little known. This is not a book about Norfolk's best churches but one which I hope will introduce you to the extraordinary range of churches the county has to offer.

Barton Bendish, St Mary

On the very edge of Breckland this is one of three churches that co-existed in this small village during the medieval period. Of the other two, St Andrew's is still in use and All Saints was demolished in the eighteenth century. St Mary's is a simple two-cell church with thatched roof that is now enjoying its retirement in the care of the Churches Conservation Trust. For such a small church there is lots of interest. When All Saints was demolished some of the materials were sold off whilst others were used to repair the other two churches, and this is where the fabulous west doorway at St Mary's came from. It is twelfth century in date and like most carved stone in this stone-poor part of Norfolk is of limestone from the area around Peterborough. The carving around the arch takes the form of beakhead decoration, designed to look like the pointed beaks of birds with boggle eyes eating the circular roll-moulding. In the centre of the door is a closing ring that is much older than the door itself. These are often overlooked but date from the days before we had moving latches. This example is probably fourteenth century. The delight of the church is that it is still thatched, one of fifty or so churches in the county that still use either reed or straw as a roof covering. Many more Norfolk churches would have originally been roofed in this form as it uses the local materials, but as thatch must be constantly renewed, most churches have at some stage invested in a more durable material. Inside, the limewashed interior is surprisingly bright. The stonework of the east window dates from around 1300 but the splashes of orange glass in its tracery are Georgian, as is the charming wooden Gothic aumbry, or cupboard, nearby. The Holy Table is an excellent example of the type of table introduced after the Reformation. It is very small and displays not only its date, 1633, but also EL, no doubt the initials of the churchwarden at the time. There are other initials carved into the top, but this is graffiti from 1782. Set into the floor of the sanctuary is a fine ledgerstone with a skull and flowing ribbons (which a previous church guidebook described as an octopus!) and a cut-down windowsill as a sedilia for the medieval clergy to use as a seat. In the nave there are the remains of a fourteenth-century wall painting depicting the wheel of fortune. There are few monuments in the church, but one to Philip Jenney, who died in 1819, is signed at the base by its sculptor, Snare of Thetford.

Bawburgh, St Mary and St Walstan

This pretty church stands on rising ground above the River Yare and has its own holy well, associated with St Walstan, a Saxon saint who became patron saint of farmers. The two gables of the nave are unique, being formed into crow-step gables of brick, set off by a jaunty cap to the round west tower. Inside, the church is obviously much loved. At the rear is an excellent example of a seventeenth-century poor box formed from a turned baluster with three hasps for the padlocks held by the parson and two churchwardens. Nearby, and often missed by visitors, is a bench end with a dedicatory inscription with the name of its sixteenth-century donor. The church displays a good royal arms of King Charles II dated 1660, painted on wooden boards and set off beautifully by its red and blue frame. The rood screen is mainly modern, but with its loft and rood beam above gives an impression of how medieval churches would have been dominated by this composition. To the north is a blocked arch which must have led into the chapel in which we know St Walstan was venerated. There is a good collection of medieval stained-glass fragments here. My favourite piece represents St Barbara and dates from the fifteenth century. She is depicted wearing a blue mantel and holds a palm branch, the symbol of martyrdom, in her right hand and the tower in which she was imprisoned (her personal symbol) in her left. In the chancel floor are several interesting brasses including one to a priest, William Richers, who died in 1531. This is of a local type made in Norwich showing a chalice of which over thirty survive in Norfolk. Nearby is Thomas Tyard (d. 1505) depicted as a very animated body in a shroud, dating from a period in history when it was fashionable to be reminded about our own mortality.

Bedingham, St Andrew

St Andrew's is a round-towered church, the tower dating from the twelfth century and showing very clear 'building lifts', the horizontal changes in stonework which represent each separate building campaign. You can count them like the rings of a tree to determine how long it took to build. The top stage of the tower is an addition of the fifteenth century when bells were hung for change ringing. It has some delicate flushwork in its blank windows. The nave is lit by a series of six clerestory windows with prominent brick relieving arches outside. Unusually the church has transepts, but no central tower. This seems to be the result of rebuilding an earlier cruciform church and has created a much larger church than one would expect. Inside, the octagonal piers of the arcades show that the aisles were added in around 1300 – so the clerestory windows above them are replacements for the originals and now date from the fifteenth century. The octagonal font is of the typical 'East Anglian' type, supported by lions and with an octagonal bowl decorated with the symbols of the Four Evangelists and a charming angel playing a lyre. The nave is full of benches of varying dates and designs. Some have carved heads on the ends whilst one has a very long dedicatory inscription to its donor. The screen is fifteenth century and is noteworthy for its delicate upper tracery and for the painted decoration on the horizontal rail comprising golden five-petalled flowers and green trailing boughs. In the south wall of the chancel there is a novel solution to the problem of how to fit sedilia, piscina and credence shelf into one composition. The sedilia, or seats for clergy, are formed in the usual way by cutting down a windowsill and the piscina (for the priest to wash his fingers) is built into its eastern end with a plain arch between the two. At the junction of the two openings is a delightful shaft of Purbeck marble. The credence (shelf) has been made into an identical feature on the western end. The church contains some interesting monuments, the finest of which is the wall tablet to William Stone who died taking the waters at Bristol in 1762.

Barton Bendish, St Mary. Exterior from the south-east showing two-cell construction and thatched roof. (Photo by Simon Knott)

Barton Bendish, St Mary. Romanesque west doorway originally in All Saints Church. (Photo by John Vigar)

Bawburgh. Exterior from the east. Note the crow-stepped gables and pyramidal cap on the round tower. (Photo by John Vigar)

Bedingham. Exterior from the south. The octagonal top was added to the round tower in the fifteenth century. (Photo by John Vigar)

Bawburgh. Fifteenth-century Norwich stained glass depicting St Barbara carrying her symbol, a tower. (Photo by John Vigar)

Bedingham. Interior with East Anglian-type font and fifteenth-century rood screen. (Photo by John Vigar)

Stained glass includes lots of medieval fragments (take binoculars) including three male saints, whilst there are Netherlandish roundels with a lot going on that were originally installed in King's College, Cambridge.

Beeston-next-Mileham, St Mary

St Mary's is an isolated church standing on a prominent ridge that is made even more a feature of the landscape on account of its tall fifteenth-century spire. Twenty years ago it seemed that this church would be lost through neglect, but in a remarkable change of fortune it has been superbly restored, winning the John Betjeman Award in the process. The atmospheric interior allows us to compare work of the fourteenth and fifteenth centuries. The oldest part is the chancel with its wonderful east window, the stonework of which is designed in the 'reticulated' style of around 1290. The nave was rebuilt around 100 years later when the walls were raised, and the clerestory windows added. One unique feature of this rebuilding was the fact that the rebuilding made the walls high enough to fit in an extra window over the chancel arch which brought even more light to illuminate the hammerbeam roof. Beneath the window is the golden painted frame to a seventeenth-century 'Godly Text', now gone. To mark the completion of the rebuilding the church was reconsecrated, and some of the circular crosses painted on the walls that were anointed by the bishop in that ceremony still survive. It is likely that the plain font is also of this date, although its tall cover is around 100 years later. The nave has chapels at each end of its aisles, each separated from the rest of the church by a medieval parclose screen. That to the north has very complex tracery along the top, whilst the south one is relatively plain. The rood screen itself has lost its top completely and looks rather strange as a result, but it is the finest piece of furniture in the church. In the spandrels of the base are a series of small carved and painted scenes including a St George and the dragon. Whilst this has been badly damaged, St George, in his gold armour with sword raised over his head, is still easy to find. The muntins (uprights) of the screen are painted in an unusual manner. Whilst many Norfolk screens have floral paintings, here there is Gothic tracery picked out in black on a gold ground, and it also incorporates initials which must be those of its donor. Looking back towards the tower you can see the original roofline marked on the west wall, which dates from before the raising of the walls and construction of the clerestory. Beneath it is a quatrefoil hole known as a hagioscope which allowed a bell ringer in the tower a view of the High Altar so that he might ring the Sanctus Bell at the appropriate time during Mass.

Belaugh, St Peter

Though not far from a main road, this feels an isolated place on a promontory of high ground encircled by the River Bure. You must want to go there, and the church is reason enough. The exterior is quite plain: a simple rectangle of nave and chancel with a north aisle and west tower. By examining the south walls, it is possible to see an interesting difference between nave and chancel. The nave is built of flint rubble, the stones being used just as they came from the fields, with large areas of mortar. The chancel on the other hand has been rebuilt and here the flints are much more tightly packed together with little mortar visible. It makes for a structurally better wall, but sadly not as interesting to look at, for the nave wall gives us lots of clues to solve. A round-headed arch shows where there was once a doorway whilst high up to the right of the porch a repair to the stonework shows where there was once a tiny window. It is also possible to pick out horizontal lines, or building lifts, delineating each phase of building work which reminds us that villagers built these early churches, fitting it into their already busy agricultural calendar. The tower is of a different building technique again where the flints have been knapped to only show their shiny black insides. Further up is the plainest of sound holes and miniscule pinnacles. Inside, everything is dominated by the rood screen, silhouetted against the light chancel. The tracery is particularly attractive for the heads are designed as a run of quatrefoil openings, as if inspired by the east window. The painted panels depict the twelve apostles and whilst they have all been damaged (literally de-faced) each is easily recognisable by their attributes. I especially like the two rather unhappy fish held by St Simon! The great authority on these paintings, Audrey Baker, pointed out something that most people would not notice: the base of the screen on the north side is painted to look like Purbeck Marble, complete with tiny fossils! Apart from the screen there are two other things to enjoy at Belaugh. Firstly, the font, which is of Norman date. It is a plain tub sitting on five pillars. Between the four outer ones are a series of round-headed arches, making it a rare design for the county. The other item of interest is a chalice brass. There are only thirty in the county, this one over the grave of John Feelde, the priest here, who died in 1508.

Booton, St Michael and All Angels

In a county known for its medieval churches, the Victorian church at Booton stands out like a sore thumb. It's not for everyone, but anyone with knowledge of architecture of that period will at once recognise it as one of the most extraordinary in England. The vision of Booton's squarson, the Revd Whitwell Elwin, it represents a rebuilding of the medieval church of which some walls and three memorials remain. Elwin was a well-known figure in nineteenth-century Britain. He was editor of the *Quarterly Review* and author of several literary works, although these pale into insignificance when his building work at Booton is studied. Most medieval churches needed major repairs in the nineteenth century, but unlike most churches Booton had, in Elwin, a man who could raise more money than was needed. Between 1875 and 1891 he worked tirelessly to create the church we see today, using money donated by his myriad of wealthy lady friends, some of whom travelled England with him as he searched for inspiration for his building works. With a flourish he took designs from churches he'd seen elsewhere and threw them together to create a cross between a college chapel and an architect's model. He was very much of the evangelical persuasion, so there is no overt symbolism here. The church is built of flint with dressed stone. Its two outlandish west towers remind me of Christopher Wren's

Beeston next Mileham. Interior looking west showing former roofline and quatrefoil hagioscope window into the tower. (Photo by Simon Knott)

Beeston next Mileham. Defaced St George on the fifteenth-century rood screen. (Photo by John Vigar)

Belaugh. Chalice brass to John Feelde, 1508. (Photo by John Vigar)

Belaugh. Fifteenth-century rood screen. (Photo by Simon Knott)

Booton. Nineteenth-century exterior from the south-east. (Photo by John Vigar)

use of Gothic after the Great Fire of London, whilst the Sanctus bell turret at the junction of nave and chancel is just for show – Elwin would never have supported such Catholic practices. Once inside it is like stepping into a barn, for the huge nave, empty of pews and dominated by a hammerbeam roof, is a tremendous space, the only homely touch being the panelling around the walls. The stained glass, by the firm of Cox, Sons and Buckley, represents musical angels rather than the more usual scenes from the life of Christ, and it is said that some of the faces are those of his supporters! In the chancel is Elwin's memorial tablet. He died on the first day of the twentieth century. Don't miss the vestry door, the label stops of which have carved woodpeckers hidden in their foliage, or the roof which has huge angels which originally held hanging lights. Booton is full of surprises.

Bracon Ash, St Nicholas

This part of Norfolk is little visited. Perhaps it's rather too close to Norwich itself, but there are many churches of interest sandwiched between the A11 and A140, of which Bracon Ash is the most characterful. It sits surrounded by trees at Bond's Green, near a medieval moated site and away from the village proper.

As you approach from the north it is obvious that this church has an excrescence attached to it. This is the eighteenth-century Berney mausoleum, a square classical single-storied building with pediment and rusticated quoins. These private extensions to churches are not uncommon but they rarely make a statement as bold as this. Perhaps it was because it would be visible from their house, Bracon Hall, that the Berneys pushed the boat out for such a statement of architectural pretension. There is no tower to this church, and we enter via a brick north porch with crow-stepped gables into a most characterful interior with honey-coloured walls and a floor of Norfolk pamments. It's only then that we realise there is a small fourteenth-century south aisle with an uncharacteristically tall arcade. On the north side of the nave the staircase to the rood loft still survives in the wall, showing that the loft was level with the capitals of the chancel arch. Above the somewhat stilted chancel arch is a large royal arms of King George III set into a classical frame. This was the traditional location for royal arms until the Victorians usually moved them somewhere less prominent, so it is good to see a set still in situ. On the opposite side of the arch, facing into the chancel, are two of a set of six funeral hatchments to be found here. It is interesting to see how the different heraldic painters interpreted their brief. The Berneys had as their crest a duke's coronet with five silver feathers, but the right-hand hatchment (for Thomas Berney, d. 1812) has much more florid feathers than that to Thomas, who had died twenty-five years earlier. The chancel itself is an unusual rebuilding of the thirteenth century. There must have been money here as the work is of high quality with the windows having elaborate hoodmoulds, even though the tracery itself is of the simplest 'Y' form, as can be seen in the east window. Around the walls are the remains of a stringcourse moulding, a standard feature of a thirteenth-century chancel, although much has been hacked off and must, at some stage, have been plastered over. There is a lovely label stop of a bishop left. In the north chancel wall are the remains of what once must have been an impressive early sixteenth-century terracotta tomb. This style was popular for a short period in the 1520s and such monuments were made from lots of separate pieces of terracotta cast in moulds and seen to best advantage at Oxborough. Unfortunately, only the surround survives here because in the eighteenth century the Berney mausoleum was built against the outside wall and the tomb chest destroyed to make a doorway into it. At the same time two thirteenth-century windows were blocked in. We do not know whose tomb this was, but the person who commissioned it must have had good connections and wanted something up to date. I'm sure lots of visitors don't even notice the terracotta work in their rush to enter the mausoleum, but it is a precious survivor. The mausoleum itself takes the form of a series of individual above ground vaults each designed to take a single coffin. Once used the vault is sealed with an inscription to the deceased. It is rare to have access to such a private space, making a visit to this church memorable.

Bressingham, St John the Baptist

St John the Baptist is an uncommonly interesting church noted for both its architecture and furnishings. The character of the church today is of the fourteenth and fifteenth centuries, the former represented by the nave and aisles, the latter by the clerestory windows and roof. The clerestory was the gift of Roger Pilkington in 1527 and leaves hardly any space for walls between the eight windows on each side. The roof coverings are interesting. Until the twentieth century responsibility for the maintenance of the nave fell to the parish and the chancel to the patron. Bressingham is a good example of each party re-roofing their part with different materials: tiles on the chancel and lead on the nave where it is also possible to see the scar of an earlier roof on the east face of the tower. Entrance is usually by the north door and the benefit of the clerestory windows is immediately clear to see in a light and lofty interior. By the door is a Gothic-style barrel organ, one of several surviving in Norfolk churches. There is also a rather grand canopied bier, for the transportation of a coffin. The font is relatively plain and dates from the fourteenth century and on each of its sides is the design for a window, as Bill Wilson writes in his Pevsner for Norfolk 'as if taken from a pattern book'. Also to be seen is a rare example of a royal arms painted on boards from the reign of Charles II, the first period when it was obligatory to display them in every parish church. The church contains a few good fragments of medieval stained glass, especially a female crowned head from the Norwich School of fifteenth-century artists. There are also excellent examples of Victorian glass, of particular note being the two windows in the north aisle by the firm of Heaton, Butler and Bayne, installed in 1865 and 1868. These were probably designed by Robert Bayne himself, known for his bold designs and use of colour. Soon after this installation the firm changed its output and moved on to less dramatic designs under the influence of Henry Holiday. In the tracery of both windows is a series of angels in a totally different style. These were probably designed by the firm of J. & J. King of Norwich who were responsible for fitting the glass. The nave is full of bench ends dating from the sixteenth century with classical arabesque figures carved on them. These represent the period of overlap between the Gothic and Classical designs, so we find religious imagery used on the finials whilst the bench ends themselves have the rather less-than-Christian arabesque as the dominant feature.

Brisley, St Bartholomew

This church is one of the few in Norfolk that has a crypt accessible to visitors. It dates from the fourteenth century and sits underneath the chancel. Entrance to it is through a small door which retains its original hinges. Originally it will have been used as a burial place and as a bone-hole, but after the Reformation it appears to have been cleared out and used as overnight accommodation for prisoners being taken from King's Lynn to Norwich! The sedilia and piscina also date from the same period, with crocketed canopies and battlemented canopy. The piscina seems rather small for the ensemble but fits perfectly. In the centre of the chancel is a remarkable brass to John Athowe, priest here who died in 1531. Sadly, he lost his head in the nineteenth century, but what survives shows craftsmanship of real quality. Nearby is an inscription to a Christopher Athowe (d. 1585), who must have been a relative. There are the remains of wall paintings throughout the church and even where full images

Bracon Ash. Exterior from the east showing the Berney mausoleum to the right. (Photo by Simon Knott)

cannot be discerned, dashes of ochre peeping out from piers and plaster tell us that something lies hidden underneath. The seating is a real hotch potch of medieval benches and box pews. One of the benches with a pierced back has an end carved with a fox running off with a goose in its mouth. High above, the roof has some interesting carvings including a prominent Devil, no doubt to dissuade evil spirits from hiding amongst the rafters. Like many Norfolk churches we know some names associated with its construction. In 1435 Robert Ediman left money to roof the porch and asked to be buried in it. This meant that worshippers would see his grave as they entered the church and remember to pray for his soul. He also left money towards building the magisterial tower with honeycomb sound holes.

Bracon Ash. Interior of the Berney mausoleum showing the loculi that line the walls, one for each burial. (Photo by John Vigar)

Bracon Ash. Sixteenth-century terracotta monument damaged by the insertion of the door into the Berney mausoleum. (Photo by John Vigar)

Right: Bressingham. Stained glass of the 1860s by Heaton, Butler and Bayne. (Photo by John Vigar)

Below: Brisley. Interior showing the ochre colour of previous decoration peeping through the limewash. (Photo by John Vigar)

Brisley. Memorial brass to the priest John Athowe, 1531. (Photo by John Vigar)

Burgh St Peter, St Mary

Church dedications make a fascinating study. This church was originally dedicated to St Peter and the 1851 Census of Religious Worship refers to it as such, so the current dedication to St Mary is a more recent dedication. This is one of the most recognisable churches in Norfolk on account of its odd brick-built west tower in the form of four brick boxes stacked on each other in diminishing size. It was built by an eighteenth-century rector, Samuel Boycott, and intended as his family mausoleum. On closer inspection it is apparent that the base is earlier. Built in flint on a grand scale, it uses brick to create an impressive diaper pattern, but it is likely that lack of funds meant that it never rose higher than you see now, waiting for its munificent eighteenth-century donor. The Boycott family provided five rectors in a row, and incidentally, the man whose name is now in common use meaning to ostracise, was the son of rector number three. The church is thatched in a single roof of nave and chancel, as is the charming porch. On the south side, the priest's door has a good Mass dial on it, used in medieval times to indicate the times of services. On the north wall of the nave is what appears to be a rectangular buttress, but this is in fact a thickening of the wall to take the staircase to the rood loft, visible internally. Inside there is a fourteenth-century font, the bowl of which is supported by some fine carved heads. The screen is nineteenth century, as is the pulpit, now covered with brass plaques commemorating successive generations of the Boycott family. However, the one thing visitors all notice is the proliferation of graffiti on the outside of the church windows. In the nineteenth and early twentieth centuries when Lowestoft and Gorleston were popular holiday destinations, this church was often the target for day excursions and visitors left their marks – thousands of them, each scratched with a diamond ring. It would be a fascinating project to research all the names and discover the human stories behind them.

Catfield, All Saints

Set on the edge of Broadland, and slightly removed from its village, Catfield is just waiting to be discovered by a wider audience. Like most of its neighbours it dates from the late medieval period, but its interest lies in the way in which it is rather different to all the others. It is a wide church with north and south aisles but was never given a clerestory, so from the outside the roof hugs the aisles like the lid on a teapot. The south porch is two storied, the room above, or parvise, is entered by a sweeping brick staircase from inside the north aisle, its junction with the aisle wall disguised by a short section of castellated wall. The lack of clerestory windows means that the centre of the church is darker than one would expect and hidden on the wall above the arcade is a splendid fourteenth-century depiction of the stoning of St Stephen. There were once other paintings, too, but they can no longer be picked out, and must always have been difficult to see, being so high up against a dark roof. The seats in the nave can truly be called pews – even though they are standard nineteenth-century benches – as they have little doors to them. These were popular for a time when our churches were being re-seated and were a halfway house between the exclusivity of rented boxes and the egalitarian principles of the church restorers. The royal arms here show a very odd feature. At the time they were painted Victoria was on the throne and her initials are prominent at the top of the canvas. However, and most unexpected, between her initials it says *1st*, as if to assume that there would be later Queen Victorias! It is the only example I've come across in England. Many tablets in the church commemorate the Cubitt family, branches of which may be found in many Norfolk villages. One of note commemorates Thomas Cubitt who was killed in the Second Anglo-Sikh War in 1848, the inscription recording that he 'met a soldier's death' at the age of twenty-four. The tablet was paid for by his fellow officers and was made by the well-known London sculptor William Groves. The most important thing to see at Catfield, however, is the rood screen, which dates from the fifteenth century, as the paintings on its base panels are rather out of the ordinary and represent a series of kings. We can see they are kings as they wear crowns, but none has a halo. It has been pointed out that the crowns are not the design that would have been worn when the screen was painted, so this was a deliberate attempt to portray the kings as historical figures. Sadly, thc ribbon texts higher on the screen above each figure, which would have been designed to take their names, were never completed, so we must guess just who they are. One holds a ring, the symbol of Edward the Confessor; another an arrow, which usually represents Edmund; whilst a third holds a Halberd, traditionally the symbol of Olaf, who was a popular saint in these parts. Apart from these it is difficult to put a name to this gallery of monarchs and much more research is needed.

Cawston, St Agnes

The western extremity of Norfolk is known for its grand churches but here at Cawston, as at its neighbour Salle, is a building that gives them a run for their money. Cathedral-like in proportion, it owes its grandeur to the munificence of the De la Pole family, Lords of the Manor here from the late fourteenth century. A large church was already here, as we can tell from the thirteenth-century architecture of the chancel and the south transept window with its beautiful early fourteenth-century tracery. Perhaps the church was being rebuilt by Michael De la Pole, Earl of Suffolk and Lord Chancellor, from east to west as was the custom, but in 1412 the west tower fell in a storm. This seems to have been the catalyst for building a new tower and nave, supported by the De La Pole family until their fall from power in 1450. Whilst they were financially generous to the church here, they were all buried elsewhere, so there are no grand monuments to discover. The tall severe tower without battlements has at its base a grand west doorway, in the spandrels of which are an enormous wodewose, or wild man of the woods, and a dragon surrounded by grape vines. We see too the shield of arms of the De La Pole family and of the Wingfields (the 2nd Earl's mother was a Wingfield). Inside the church its glory is a hammerbeam roof, dating from the late fifteenth century and one of the finest in England. By this date the power of the De la Poles had passed, but the work they had started was continued by other donors. The angels on the end of each hammerbeam retain much of their original colour, and from the ground it is not easy to realise that they are human size. Between them on the wall plates are rather more conventional angels whose bodies are tiny compared to their outstretched wings. Above the chancel arch are the remains of red wall paintings in which the shape of the cross, or rood, which stood against the wall may still be seen, together with the location of the heads of the statues of Our Lady and St John. The screen itself is around the same date as the roof and along the base there is an inscription asking us to pray for the donors, who were William and Alice Atereth. The figures were painted by three different artists, one of whom painted their images on vellum which was then pasted to the panels, rather than directly onto the wood. The muntins of the screen have applied gesso in a Gothic tracery pattern, here and there incorporating tiny slivers of glass to make it more splendid (use the torch on your phone to find them). The figures are not as damaged as most screens, with the majority just having a scratched cross over the face. My favourite image is of St Matthew wearing some very fetching spectacles. The chancel is relatively plain compared to the nave, and its roof is a somewhat simpler delight.

Burgh St Peter. The unique brick tower intended as the Boycott mausoleum. (Photo by Simon Knott)

Burgh St Peter. Graffiti inscriptions left by trippers cover the windows. (Photo by John Vigar)

Catfield. Exterior from the south. (Photo by John Vigar)

Catfield. One of the kings on the fifteenth-century rood screen – probably St Olaf of Norway.

Cawston. Chancel roof. (Photo by Matthew McDade)

Cawston. Carved angel on the wall plate. (Photo by Matthew McDade)

Cawston. St Matthew wears glasses on the fifteenth-century rood screen. (Photo by John Vigar)

CLEY-NEXT-THE-SEA, ST MARGARET

Situated where there was once a busy port on Blakeney Haven, this church proclaims the wealth and confidence of the early fourteenth century. Financed by merchants, it is unlike most Norfolk churches which date from a century later, making this a stand-alone study. The tracery of the ruined south transept south window is an accomplished design based on two huge quatrefoils, whilst the clerestory is based on circles with cinquefoils. With comparatively little architecture of this period surviving in the county, it strikes the visitor as fresh and alive. Only the later porch is typically Norfolk, built in the Perpendicular Gothic style with its vertical windows and elaborately pierced parapet. Most of the church is built of flint rubble, but the porch is ashlar – expensive dressed stone – and it is here that legal and financial transactions were conducted, in the sight of God but not part of the church. Two bosses in its roof are completely secular in nature, one showing a woman chasing a fox which has stolen her hen, the other a naughty person having their bare bottom spanked. We enter the church through an early fourteenth-century doorway with splendid ogee arch, into an impressive space. It must originally have been even more so, as between the arcades are elaborate brackets on which colourful statues would have stood, with a complicated canopy over each. On careful inspection you can see where the heads of some of these statues came on the wall, which must have been replastered around them. The font dates from the late fifteenth century and is of the familiar Seven Sacrament type, although the iconography is uncommon. My friend Simon Knott (www.norfolkchurches.co.uk) points out that in the scene of the Last Rites it looks as if the administering priest is lying on top of the dying person! In every scene we can certainly say that the sculptor was an expert in carving hair. The benches in the nave have some varied carvings of animals and people, although some have been recut with new faces. The church contains many minor monuments which include a set of sixteenth-century brasses and a tablet to John Winn Thomlinson who died on Boxing Day 1835 in 'a fit of apoplexy'.

Cranwich, St Mary

One of the simplest Norfolk churches, St Mary's stands in an isolated Breckland landscape. Its enchanting setting is just right for a church that evokes another, simpler, age. The round tower is one of the few that dates from before the Norman Conquest, and has very clear horizontal lines representing the building lifts. Just above the roofline there is an ornate sound hole, carved from a single piece of stone in a knot-like design, a horizontal line just above this marking the extent of the original tower. The church is thatched – nave, chancel and south porch. There is no show or pretension here at all, two late medieval windows face south from the nave whilst two thirteenth-century windows with 'Y' tracery light the chancel. You enter via a late Norman doorway with the plainest of mouldings into an interior which is completely limewashed, walls and ceilings. At the back the nave has some open wooden benches, whilst nearer the front we find more solid benches with *fleur de lys* ends. Dominating the east wall are the Creed, Lord's Prayer and Ten Commandments, as required by law until the mid-nineteenth century. The font is a plain structure of the fourteenth century and the floor delightfully uneven, showing us that the Victorians had a very light touch here. Monuments are thin on the ground in such a poor area but there is a ledger slab of Jane Hayward (d. 1633). The slab tells us who her father and husband were but forgets to tell us how old she was when she died. A blank had been left on the stone, but nobody filled it in. Another query arises when we look at the War Memorial. It is headed 'Men of Cranwich who served abroad 1914-1918' and lists twelve men. However, they are divided into two distinct groups without making it clear that the first four were casualties, the rest returnees. Nearby is a flat slab with small crosses incised into it that must have been the mensa, or altar slab, in pre-Reformation times. On the wall is a tablet to an early nineteenth-century rector, John Partridge.

East Harling, St Peter and St Paul

One of the most interesting churches in Norfolk, St Peter and St Paul's sits well on a mound high over the village street, the tower with its crown spirelet adding a rather oriental feel. Here is a substantial church of the thirteenth and fourteenth centuries that was given a makeover by Anne Harling and her two husbands in the fifteenth century. The interior seems surprisingly narrow but very tall with a series of nine clerestory windows flooding the interior with light. Above the chancel arch is a ventilation hole to the chancel roof and above that a window that would, in a smaller church, be adequate for a main east window! On the north wall of the chancel, and open to the vestry behind, is the massive tomb of Sir William Chamberlain (d. 1462), the first husband of Anne Harling. It takes the form of an Easter sepulchre; its flat top being used for part of the Easter ritual. The carving is very fine, and the whole must have looked stunning when it was painted, the shields along the front dazzling in their display of heraldry. Even without the colouring you can pick out the emblem of a Knight of the Garter around the edge of the arch itself, Sir William being rewarded for long service in the wars against France. Above the monument his shield is, once again, encircled by the Garter. Chamberlain was also responsible for setting up a chapel in the south aisle to his wife's parents. This part of the church is fascinating and contains many wonders. Sir Robert Harling and his wife are commemorated by the elaborate arched alcove next to the south chapel altar, the detail of which is delightful. Two of the symbols of the family were the unicorn and the *fleur de lys* and you can find these carved around the edge of the cusped arch. There is another unusual device to be seen on the tomb: a woven basket with two handles. These have been much debated over the years with suggestions ranging from a workman's tool carrier to a flail used for winnowing corn, but I prefer to go with the theory that they are herring baskets. By the fifteenth century herrings were one of the main sources of income in the county. The two alabaster effigies under the arch don't belong to it. They are Harlings from the century before, moved here in a subsequent tidy-up. Next to them is a much more impressive monument, a multi-coloured confection supported by six huge pillars. Here is Sir Thomas Lovell (d. 1604) and his wife, at his feet the family crest of a bundle of peacock feathers. At her feet is the Huddlestone crest of a scalp, the story of which originates with an ancestor who was imprisoned during the crusades but who escaped when his long hair tied to a beam was cut, together with his scalp! I love the details on this monument – her signet ring is life-size and so realistic you feel you could just take it off. In the chancel are two monuments to sixteenth-century Lovells, two heraldic 'sideboards' with no effigies or religious symbolism. Here too is the great glory of this church, for the east window is full of high-quality fifteenth-century glass. How it survived the iconoclasm of the sixteenth and seventeenth centuries in unclear but here it is, scenes from the Life of Christ in eighteen rectangular panels, and most certainly made in Norwich. Again, it is full of detail, and in the two bottom corner panels are portraits of the kneeling donors, the two husbands of Anne Harling. Do take binoculars to appreciate the details of this national treasure. The church also contains several exceptional wooden screens. The best separates the south chapel from its aisle and is complete with a loft and just a little piece of original cresting. Look for the unicorns of the Harlings above the entrance to the chapel, but also the delightful dragons and faces carved along the bottom panels. At the back of the church are the base panels from the screen that originally separated nave and chancel, one of which has a remarkable carving of the Tree of Jesse with the vine issuing from Jesse's stomach and ending in what would have been the crucified Christ before the iconoclasts got to him.

Cley next the Sea. Porch roof boss depicting a woman chasing a fox. (Photo by John Salmon)

Cley next the Sea. Exterior from the south-west showing the ruined south transept. (Photo by John Vigar)

East Harling. Norwich stained glass depicting The Ascension. (Photo by John Vigar)

East Harling. Owl hidden in the parclose screen to the south chapel. (Photo by John Vigar)

East Ruston. A devil has its life extinguished by the weight of the font. (Photo by John Vigar)

East Ruston. Probably a portrait of the donor on one side of the font. (Photo by John Vigar)

East Ruston, St Mary

One of the county's retired churches and in the care of the Churches Conservation Trust, St Mary's sits beside the road with its only neighbour the Old Rectory, the gardens of which are much celebrated and open to the public. In many ways it embodies what Norfolk churches are all about, a tale of medieval grandeur, decline, neglect and survival against the odds. What we see today is a church built of flint of two types: the more usual field flints with straight edges, and flint cobbles collected from the beach and rounded by the sea. The latter are more difficult to use as there is not much opportunity for them to key to the mortar. When the north aisle was lost in 1778 it was replaced by a red-brick wall, making it an enormous visual contrast for the visitor circumnavigating the church for the first time. Impressive as it seems today, St Mary's must have been even more so before it lost its spire. The tower on which it stood is of fourteenth-century date, which is the same as the south aisle. A horizontal band of dressed stone, or stringcourse, runs around them both, but stops before it gets to the chancel south wall, which was already there. The top of the tower has some characterful water spewers on the corner. To the north of the tower are some foundations of a substantial building which it is thought were once a free-standing chapel dedicated to Our Lady and mentioned in medieval wills. The church is usually entered today via the chancel door and brings you into a very Victorianised part of the building, reminding us that until the twentieth century these two parts of the building were in separate ownership. In 1887 the patron, responsible for the chancel, refitted it to include a new floor and furnishings. Some of the roof here uses old timbers but you can see the corbels that the original roof sat on poking out of the walls. Once you move towards the nave you see that, apart from the ceiling which was installed after the north aisle had been demolished, we are in a relatively untouched medieval structure. The joy here is the rood screen. Although it was damaged at the Reformation by having its loft removed, it remains one of great interest. Firstly, there is a carved lion sitting on a little castellated bracket guarding the entrance to the chancel. Its mane still shows traces of the golden colour with which it was originally painted. Only one other Norfolk screen is known to have had this feature. The muntins (uprights) to the screen are painted in a floral scheme which is continued up into the tracery above. This is made rather more elaborate than usual by having two distinct carved sets of tracery, one on each side of the screen to give a three-dimensional effect. The eight painted panels of the screen are not artistically of high quality but are very little damaged so worthy of close inspection. They are each labelled in a ribbon text, showing us that on the north side they represent the Four Evangelists and on the south side by the Four Latin Doctors of the church. St Luke looks a particularly charming old gent, whilst St Mark's lion certainly has a mind of his own! On the other side Jerome is easily identified by his cardinal's hat whilst St Augustine, with his multi-ringed hand, looks as though he has badly applied lipstick. These locally produced works of art are just as important as those of metropolitan quality. At the back of the church is the fourteenth-century font, octagonal as usual and displaying again the Four Evangelists with three bearded men. The eighth side, facing down the church, is the odd one out, and I think must depict the donor of the font, for he is unshaven and looks to be of the right period with a very natty hairdo. At the base of the font are demons, the life being forced out of them by the weight of the font and its symbolism as a power for good. These carvings were all recut in 1882 but followed the original design.

Edingthorpe, All Saints

A favourite church of many, All Saints in Edingthorpe stands well away from its village on higher ground reached by a narrow lane. Its beauty lies in its simplicity of round tower, thatched nave and small tiled chancel. The tower is Norman, with easy-to-see building lifts, although it telescopes into a fourteenth-century octagonal top added at a time when bells became more common. A will refers to this work in 1357. The south door is medieval with its original ring pull but there is a second, older door mounted on the west wall inside. This was the medieval north door, recently replaced. The interior is light and barn-like, the effect enhanced by the fact that the nineteenth-century roof of the chancel is entirely limewashed. The chancel arch is tall and it is interesting to see the gap between the top of the screen and the springing of the arch which represents the location of the walkway on top of the loft. Cut into the stonework are holes and niches that would have held the wooden structure. In the north wall of the nave the upper doorway to the loft can be clearly seen. The lower doorway has an amazing painted niche above it which must once have held a large statue. The screen itself is one of the earliest in Norfolk, dating from the fourteenth century. The circular whorls above the central doorway are delicately carved. The panels themselves are of great interest. When the screen was first erected it was not the fashion to decorate them with images, and this one was painted red with white *fleur de lys* over the top. In the fifteenth century, when the custom of painting figures had become widespread, six figures were painted over the top of the original scheme and as the panels didn't have carved tracery tops, these too were painted on in white paint. In the figure of St Peter (holding a key) you can see the *fleur de lys* peeping through from underneath whilst in the figure of Bartholomew you can clearly see that the white paint of the tracery goes over the edge of his halo. The church also displays some fine medieval wall paintings. The best preserved is a figure of St Christopher carrying a rather large Christ child. It is high on the wall so had to be large to enable medieval parishioners to pick it out. Nearby are the faint remains of a painting of the Seven Works of Mercy, of which feeding the hungry is the easiest scene to pick out. The seventeenth-century pulpit has a wrought-iron stand for an hourglass and the reading desk is dated 1537.

Erpingham, St Mary

In a county where there are so many church towers peppering the landscape it is very common to become disorientated and to wonder which church you're looking at. No chance at Erpingham where the name is emblazoned on the top of the tower for all to see! Along the base of the tower are a series of shields recording the families who donated towards the work in 1485 including Erpingham, Latimer and Boleyn. The other interesting feature to see outside is the tiny bellcote at the junction of nave and chancel. This housed the Sanctus bell which would have been rung at the Consecration during Mass. Thirty-one of these survive in Norfolk. Inside, the floor is covered with local pamments, punctuated by memorials and ledger slabs, the most important of which is a brass to Sir John Erpingham who died in 1370. It is by a London workshop and was probably paid for by his son, the famous Sir Thomas Erpingham, hero of Agincourt and benefactor of Norwich Cathedral where he is buried. Between the south aisle and chancel is a large hagioscope, or window. This would have served an altar which stood in front of it and allowed its officiating priest to coordinate his service with the one taking place at the main altar. The bases of the piers between the aisle and nave are not at floor level and would have provided perches for weary parishioners at a time before seating came in, hence the expression, 'the weak go to the wall'. There is a fair amount of stained glass in the church, some of it medieval and collected by a former rector, but it is the east window that attracts most attention. It is a copy of continental glass of the 1520s that has an interesting story. In the early nineteenth century a Norwich dealer specialised in selling continental glass to wealthy customers and the window was purchased from him and installed at Blickling Hall. In 1955 it was removed and installed here only to be taken back in the 1990s when this copy was made for the church. Because the panels came from elsewhere, they didn't fill the window completely, so the gaps are filled with what are known as 'Venetian roundels'. You can see a scene in the top row that shows a similar window which gave the inspiration here.

FRENZE, ST ANDREW

This church packs more of a punch than its diminutive size would suggest. All that survives today is the nave of a two-cell medieval church which lost its chancel in 1820. The church has hardly been touched since. The pulpit is a fine early seventeenth-century affair with decorative pendants dripping from its sounding

Edingthorpe. Detail of the delicate rood screen tracery. (Photo by John Vigar)

Edingthorpe. Interior looking east. (Photo by Simon Knott)

Edingthorpe. Wall painting depicting St Christopher. (Photo by John Vigar)

Frenze. Exterior showing the surviving nave of a two-cell church. (Photo by John Vigar)

Frenze. Early seventeenth-century private box pew. (Photo by John Vigar)

Fritton. Exterior from the south-east. (Photo by David Striker)

Fritton. Painting of the Bacon family on the Rood Screen. (Photo by John Vigar)

Fritton. Unfinished panel on the south side of the rood screen.

board and overlooking the private pew of the owners of Frenze Hall. This, too, is seventeenth century, with turned balusters to give a view out and decorative panels in the lower sections. Sadly, in an incomplete state are the royal arms, for they too date from the same period and are for James I – an early date for Norfolk churches. Fragments of earlier glass and a lovely fourteenth-century font with blank window tracery carved on its sides complete the furnishings, but it is the large collection of memorial brasses that one really comes to see. They mostly commemorate the family from the big house and cover a period of a hundred years. The earlier ones have inscriptions in Latin, but as they run into the sixteenth century the inscriptions are increasingly in English. Two stick in the memory. A widow, Johanna Braham (d. 1519), is shown as a *religious* – in other words she has pledged not to remarry and to live a religious life without joining a monastic community. Thomas Hobson (d. 1520) is shown in his shroud with his eyes closed in prayer. Nearby a later inscription directs us to the family burial place with the stark words 'Vault's Mouth'.

Fritton, St Catherine

There are two Frittons in Norfolk and this one is near Hempnall in as a remote location, as can be imagined. Reached via a bowered track, this round-towered church is entered by a medieval door with its original closing ring, and the remains of a dedicatory inscription across its transom. Inside we are in a single rectangular space, separated into nave and chancel by a rood screen and it is this that we have come to see. Because it is a small church the screen is not as impressive as many, but its paintings are most interesting. Firstly, an inscription running across the left-hand panels tell us that this was the gift of John Bacon – and there he is with his large family of ten sons and three daughters, each holding their rosary. It is the ultimate in donor scenes. Their costumes show a degree of wealth, from his black vest to their fur-lined capes. Next to them are the four doctors of the church. On the other side of the screen things get even more interesting. The screens were constructed over a period and then painted in situ by a travelling artist. For some reason the screen was never finished. Perhaps money ran out to finish the final pieces of carving, but whatever the reason the artist turned up to paint the panels only to find that two of them had not been carved. His solution was simple – to make the best of a bad job and paint fictive tracery on the uncarved portions. It is the only known example of its type and reminds us of the complexity of commissioning a piece of furniture in the medieval period. Nearby, and painted on the wall, is a small figure of St Edmund of Abingdon, painted in the thirteenth century when his cult was at its peak. Like many lesser saints he was soon forgotten in favour of the greats, so this is a rare find.

Great Cressingham, St Michael

St Michael's is a magnificent church which dominates the centre of this sprawling village. It differs from its neighbours in that it is the result of only a partial rebuild of the fifteenth century. The chancel is still late thirteenth century, its exterior beautified by two pinnacles sprouting like rockets from ashlar buttresses either side of the east window. Whilst the latter is obviously a later insertion, the side windows of the chancel are original. This shows that the patrons of churches, who were responsible only for the chancel, were not always in step with the parishioners in matching their individual building campaigns. That this tension survived until recent times can be shown by the fact that the chancel is roofed in slate, whilst the nave is of tile. Here the chancel was left as built but in the fifteenth century the nave was substantially rebuilt, and a tower and porch added. In an age when most building work was by unknown craftsmen, it is thought that the work here was undertaken by James Woderofe who also worked at Norwich, Wymondham and Eton. This work was completed by the construction of a fine hammerbeam roof. As well as the usual angels on both the hammer beams and wall posts there are some priestly figures, too, especially noticeable where the roof meets the east wall of the nave above the chancel arch. Here, giving adoration to the rood beneath that has long since disappeared, are two figures whose bodies are turned to the rood and whose hands are separated in a pose of adoration. When they were brightly painted, they must have looked stunning. Medieval colour survives in plenty in the north aisle where much stained glass remains in the tracery heads. They represent angels, bishops and three fragments from the Mystery of the Rosary. Take binoculars because they are very high up and the beauty is in the detail. There is a venerable wooden domed chest, one of 130 to survive in England, imported from Poland in the fifteenth century and a fine set of brasses. A wall tablet recalls two sad deaths of children of a nineteenth-century rector. One died whilst a student at Oxford, another aged just twenty-two weeks. If you look closely at the bottom of the inscription you'll see that the letter carver made quite a botch of it!

HALES, ST MARGARET

St Margaret's is without doubt one of the most famous Norman churches in the county, now in the safe hands of the Churches Conservation Trust. It has been visited by travellers for centuries, who recognised it as a good example of early church architecture. The first thing that strikes the visitor is that it has a thatched roof, as many churches would have had originally. Secondly, it has a contemporary round tower and thirdly, its east end is rounded into the form of an apse. A walk around the exterior is most rewarding. The main north doorway is as elaborate as a rural Norman church could muster, of five orders with zigzag and bobbin mouldings. The tower displays the now familiar horizontal building lifts representing each season's work. There is a nicely carved south doorway, too, with some grotesque decoration. To its right is a blocked Norman window between two later and larger replacements. Once we reach the apse, we see the wealth of dressed stonework in the arcading at high level around the walls. Not all these arches were windows; most were purely for decoration. Today they are punctuated by inserted thirteenth-century windows, but you get the feeling that without them the apse would be even more impressive. Inside the church are some fragments of medieval wall painting, the finest being a fictive image canopy over a square recess in a north window. More survive in the chancel. The rood screen has been cut down, but the base panels still have traces of the original red and green painted backgrounds. The church contains few memorials but a ledgerstone in the chancel attracts attention. It covers the grave of Peter Lawes, rector here who died in 1722. To show his learning his inscription is in Latin. However, when his widow died thirty-one years later at the grand age of ninety-nine, her inscription was added in English!

HARDLEY, ST MARGARET

This corner of Norfolk is known for the diversity of its churches, which goes to show how localised medieval wealth was. This squat little church overlooking the marshes has a Norman round tower with Tudor battlements that make it look rather like a toy fort. As you step down into the church your eyes are taken to the enormous painting of St Christopher on the wall. Dating from the fifteenth century, it shows that the north door was always the main one, as people on their way to work would pop their heads around the door to see the image, for they believed that this would ensure they had a safe day. For this reason, St Christopher images are almost always opposite the main door. I love the fish swimming between his legs and the heron looking up at the Christ child.

Great Cressingham. Memorial brass to William Eyre, 1509. (Photo by John Vigar)

Unusually the painting was made to look as if it was painted on a canvas sheet hung on the wall – it has a thick grapevine border and an ermine background to differentiate it from the surrounding wall. To its right, and a separate painting, is a small image of St Catherine holding her wheel which is slightly earlier. On the west wall a very prominent consecration cross survives. This was one of twelve painted crosses that would have been anointed with oil by the bishop when the church was consecrated. Two pieces of carved stonework are of note. The font is of the typical East Anglian type, the bowl being supported by elongated lions. In the chancel the piscina is set into a highly carved ogee-headed arch. It is still possible to pick out traces of its original paint. The church appears to be full of Georgian pine benches, but on close inspection this is just an external cladding to the original medieval benches. The tell-tale is the huge step into the benches which is still the medieval frame into which the medieval seats are slotted. This hybrid arrangement would usually have been replaced by the Victorian restorers but the church here wasn't doing very well at the time as most villagers attended the Wesleyan Chapel, and consequently very little repair work was undertaken, resulting in an interior of great charm.

Hales. The rare apsidal east end and thatched roof. (Photo by John Vigar)

Great Cressingham. Hammerbeam roof in the nave. (Photo by John Vigar)

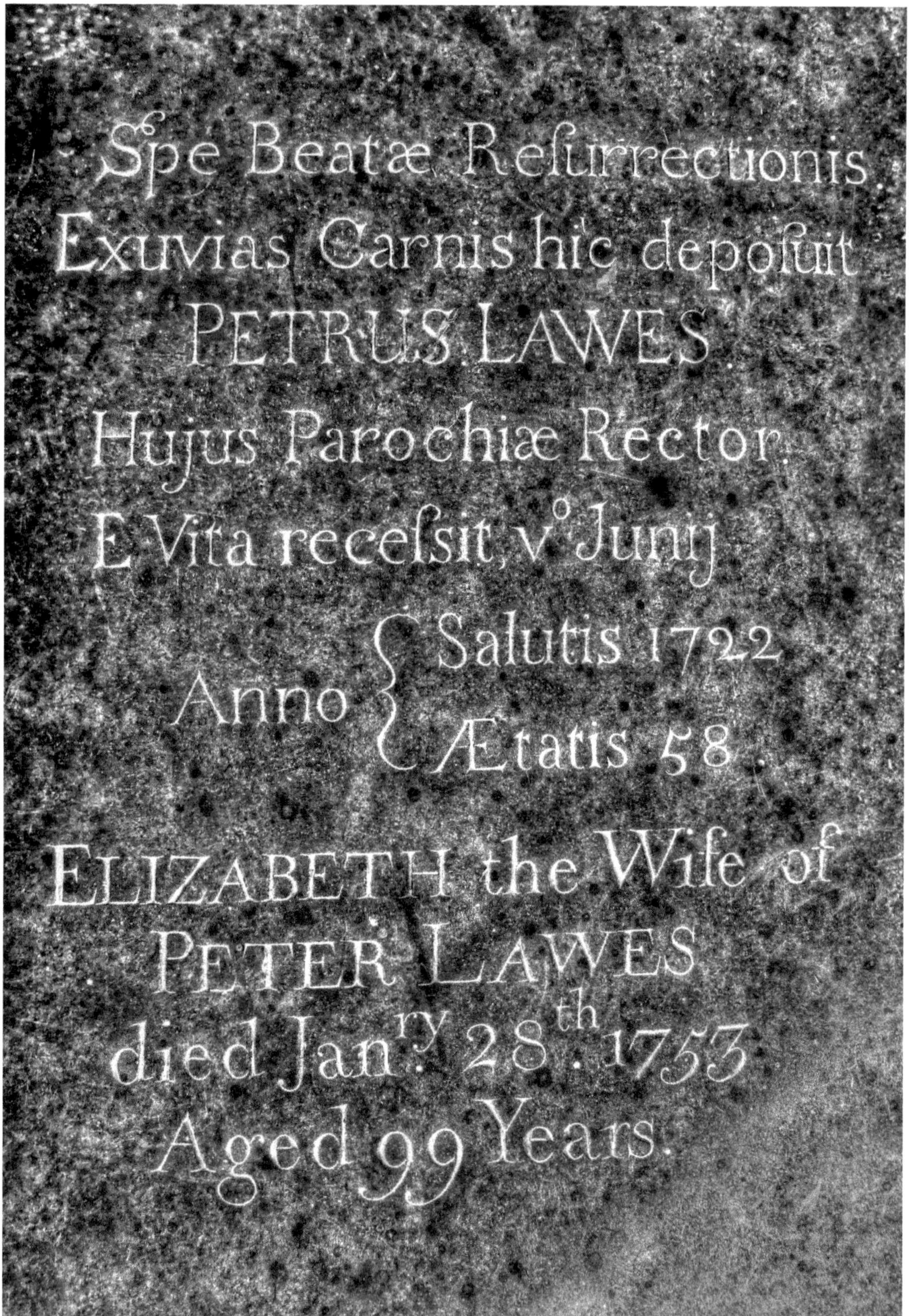

Hales. Eighteenth-century ledgerstone to Elizabeth and Peter Laws. (Photo by John Vigar)

Hales. Capital on Romanesque north doorway.

Hardley. Round-towered church with later battlements viewed from the south. (Photo by John Vigar)

Hardley. Medieval benches turned into box pews by the addition of pine cladding. (Photo by John Vigar)

Harpley St Lawrence

When a church was founded or substantially rebuilt by a single benefactor that person was usually given pride of place for his subsequent burial. This was invariably in the chancel, and the visitor to Harpley today cannot fail to see the enormous slab in the floor covering the grave of John de Gurney. His brass has been lost, but even so it is a majestic piece. Gurney rebuilt the chancel in the early fourteenth century complete with sedilia and double piscina and an even more impressive doorway leading to the vestry. One hundred years later the nave was rebuilt by the addition of aisles, clerestory, west tower and porch. This time it was not funded by a single benefactor, but by a group of individuals whose shields of arms can be seen on the parts of the building they paid for, the best example being outside on the south aisle parapet. The main south door is one of the most important in the county, carved with the usual blank tracery but also with images of the Four Doctors of the church and the Four Evangelists. It must have been splendid when covered in colour. Entrance is via a small wicket door in the centre which takes you into a light interior. The benches have poppy head ends and pretty pierced tracery backs whilst the roof has unusually animated angels running east to west along its apex. The screen is mostly medieval but unfortunately the garish painting is all Victorian. By the exuberant nineteenth-century font you'll find some interesting graffiti scratched onto the clear glass window.

Hemblington, All Saints

All Saints, Hemblington, is an unforgettable small, round-towered church in an isolated position east of Norwich. The two features that bring us here are both items of colour. Most important are the fourteenth-century wall paintings which show not just St Christopher but also scenes from his life as described in *The Golden Legend*. There are lots of small scenes, so binoculars would be useful, but his attempted execution is large enough to see without. Christopher was tied to a tree and shot with arrows, but as the legend relates, those that hit him bounced off, and one particularly nasty arrow has clearly done just that. Having failed to kill him in that manner he was finally beheaded. The other reason to come here is to see the font which dates from the fifteenth century. It depicts a collection of saints, mostly identifiable by their emblems, but what makes it really special is the way in which it is painted. Most fonts would have looked like this when new, but few retain any paint at all. In the 1930s the surviving colour was conserved by Professor Tristram, the doyen of medieval art, and lightly touched up. The church also boasts many brass inscription plates, mostly in Latin, but my favourite is the one in English to Rebeka Howlet who died in 1630, as the lettering is exquisite.

Heydon, St Peter and St Paul

Heydon is one of those chocolate-box villages that grew up serving a large estate and which seems remote from the modern world. The church dominates the village green, especially by its tall west tower which dates from the later fifteenth century. It is one of those churches where the scale of the place is all powerful, and this really is a specialist church, worth devoting an hour or two to explore, as it is full of unusual treasures. The fifteenth-century pulpit is of the wine glass shape, sitting on a stone pedestal. Its rustic feel should be compared to the seventeenth-century sounding board which is altogether more refined. The rood screen is of the same date and decorated with the alternating red and green design along the base and barber-pole decoration up the mullions. On top of the south end of the screen is an inscription telling us that this was given by John Dyne in 1480. The north end of the screen is pretty much hidden by one of two private family pews in the church, this one dating from the late seventeenth century. Hanging in the north aisle are two funeral helms – stage prop helmets carried at the funerals of armigerous men in the sixteenth and seventeenth centuries. As the fashion for wearing armour declined so did the use of helms at funerals, to be replaced by hatchments. There are four of these in the church, each painted on canvas and stretched in a diamond-shaped frame. As an estate church, Heydon contains many memorials to the families from the hall and their connections which were fixed to blank areas of wall. What was not known at the time was that underneath the limewash medieval wall paintings survived! These were discovered in the 1970s and subsequently uncovered. Today it is apparent how much damage was caused when the monuments were placed over them, but enough paintings survive to show us what they once depicted. The most famous shows the medieval legend of the *Three Living and Three Dead*, a morality tale about three princes going hawking and coming across three skeletons who reminded them that one day all their wealth would mean nothing. Sadly, not only did memorials get slapped on them but one prince got destroyed when a window was cut into the wall. Nevertheless, the two surviving noblemen look suitably surprised and their hawk flaps its wings as if startled too. At the end of the aisle is a sequence of paintings representing scenes from the life of St John the Baptist. These are not as easy to see, but you can pick out Salome dancing in front of King Herod. In a better state of preservation, we can see part of a Nativity scene with the Three Kings presenting their offerings.

HICKLING, ST MARY

Whilst Hickling is best known for its expansive Broad, the countryside and villages around its edge are a testament to medieval agriculture, each church a microcosm in stone of local history. St Mary's stands back from its village centre in a large churchyard, its tall four-stage tower with square sound holes looking even taller than it is. It is interesting as the putlog holes, where the wooden scaffolding was inserted in the walls as they were built, have been retained, the dressed stone in complete contrast to the flint rubble of the walls. This is particularly evident in the lower stages where the flints are arranged to show their shiny black insides, and although the putlog holes are visible to the very top, they are less evident in the rubble-built upper stages. The slate roof to the church tells you that this church had a thorough going over in the nineteenth century and that is very much the feeling once you get inside with black and red glazed tiles running throughout the building. The pulpit is a very odd affair, joined to the wall by a little jetty, with a returning staircase facing the nave. At the back of the church is a rather good early nineteenth-century parish bier with wooden canopied roof, and an unusual fourteenth-century font with alternate blank tracery and foliate faces. However, the two outstanding features of the church are both monuments. The

Harpley. A church blessed with many late medieval benefactors. (Photo by Gary J. Brothwell)

Harpley. Interior showing ventilation to chancel roof, octagonal piers and repainted screen. (Photo by Gary J. Brothwell)

Harpley. The finest medieval door in Norfolk. (Photo by John Vigar)

Hemblington. A small round-towered church whose simple exterior belies the treasures within. (Photo by Aidan McRae Thomson)

Hemblington. Medieval wall painting from the Life of St Christopher. (Photo by John Vigar)

Hickling. The rectangular opening in the tower is a Norfolk sound hole. (Photo by Simon Knott)

Hickling. Hand and feet graffiti on a chest tomb dates from the seventeenth and eighteenth centuries. (Photo by John Vigar)

first is a thirteenth-century grave cover with moulded sides that carries on its top a floriate cross and an inscription in Lombardic lettering. The second is the plain chest tomb with no inscription and plain shields on the side. What makes this notable is the enormous amount of graffiti scratched on its flat surface. Firstly, there are the familiar outlines of feet and hands left by people who just wanted to make their mark. Then there are the board games, such as Nine Men's Morris, often to be found on flat surfaces in medieval churches. The most interesting finds here date from the time of the English Civil War, with one inscription recording 'Roundheade 1645'. At the time this was a derisory term, so possibly scratched by a Royalist to record some village incident surrounding a Puritan? It seems we will never know.

HINDRINGHAM, ST MARTIN

The fourteenth-century tower of this church seems exceptionally tall as it has no string courses until you reach the bell stage and stands on high ground. Its bell openings have delicately designed tracery, which is mirrored in the great east window, although the stonework there is of nineteenth-century date. The church itself was substantially rebuilt in the fifteenth century creating a light and wide interior, although the rebuilding changed the axis of the building so that the central gangway no longer lines up with the centre of the chancel. Whilst this is a common medieval feature it is rather more obvious here than in many churches. To the left of the chancel arch is the doorway that originally lead onto the rood loft. Unusually it faces east-west rather than the usual north-south configuration, which means that the chancel arch is set to the south in order to accommodate it. The font is rather unusual in its iconography. Its central theme is the Crucifixion, although, unsurprisingly, that scene was damaged by the iconoclasts. The next panel depicts the Instruments of the Passion in great detail including the ladder, dice, nails and spear. Then follow the symbols of the Four Evangelists and the Trinity whilst the final panel shows the royal arms of England as they were when we used the *fleur de lys* of France. There are fragments of medieval stained glass which show how glorious the interior once must have been. In one an angel plays the lute whilst in another the angel holds a star to his chest – an image which may be found elsewhere in Norfolk. There are some good floor monuments in the church, including one to the potter Peter Temple-Richards who died in 1975. The highlight of a visit to Hindringham, though, is the church chest, which is one of the oldest in England, dating from the late thirteenth century. Its front is decorated with the familiar intersecting tracery of the Romanesque period, though the chest is considerably later, as proved by recent dendrochronological study. It is frequently the case that medieval woodworkers were often two or three generations behind stonemasons in giving up much-loved forms of decoration. As no other early chests survive in parish churches it is assumed that this one didn't originate here and found a home in St Martin's during a later period, possibly in the sixteenth century when every church was ordered to have one.

HOLKHAM, ST WITHBURGA

This church stands within the park of Holkham Hall and has benefitted from more than one rebuild generously paid for by the Coke family. It is accessible all year by parking in the village car park, walking into the park and turning right immediately inside the gate. It is a delightful 25-minute walk. For an estate church it is surprisingly not the main family burial place, that privilege resting with Tittleshall where the family originated. However, their influence is seen everywhere here, and the church contains memorials to many generations of local folk. It stands on what was once a sand dune, the sea coming right past this hill and well into the park until landscape improvements pushed it over a mile away. Not that you would realise any of this just by looking at its verdant setting, with an odd Victorian mausoleum half in and half out of the churchyard. From the earliest church date two thirteenth-century coffin lids. One has a double-omega design, often taken as a sign that it came from Barnack in the far corner of Cambridgeshire, one of several dozen to survive in eastern England. The Wheatley Monument of 1639 shows fifteen children along the base, five of whom have turned their heads as if the sculptor had said something to surprise them! A sad ledgerstone marks the grave of the still-born son of Sir Nicholas Lestrange (1658) whilst another records the death at the age of five of Susan Doyly, a great heiress. But the monument that everyone remembers here is that to Juliana, Second Countess of Leicester, who rebuilt the church in its present incarnation in 1869. She lies in cool white marble, on a tomb chest carved by Queen Victoria's favourite sculptor, Sir Joseph Boehm. Often visitors will improve on the design by adding a posy of flowers on her chest. A bright orange stained-glass window records work to the previous church by her predecessor in 1768.

King's Lynn, St Nicholas Chapel

Of the three surviving medieval churches in Lynn this is the finest architecturally, and it comes as a surprise to visitors to realise that this was never a parish church. Given its grandeur, and the fact that it contains a mayoral mace rest one would assume it was the main civic church, but it was always a chapel in the parish of the Minster. Built in the early fifteenth century and now in the care of the Churches Conservation Trust, it is a popular venue for concerts and shows. The west window is one of the largest ever built in a lesser church and is perhaps more impressive today now that it is filled with plain glass. The west door sticks up into it to create a single composition, its original door having recently been repainted in its original colours of red and green. Inside the font and its Victorian cover dominates the west end and tucked into one corner is a rare Consistory Court where the Chancellor of the Diocese once sat to hear cases in this far-flung part of west Norfolk. The interior is one large rectangle, with one of the finest angel roofs in the country. The chapel contains one of the rare medieval eagle lecterns which the Victorians so much liked to copy. It is supported by four tiny lions and whilst the eagle has its beak open this was never (as is commonly suggested) a money box, as when they were first made in the early sixteenth century they would have stood in the chancel, away from the congregation. There is another in the Minster. The monuments in the chapel commemorate those merchants connected with the North End of the town and benefactors. Outstanding amongst them is the oval monument designed by Robert Adam for Benjamin Keene (d. 1757), British Consul in Madrid. No doubt he was introduced to Adam by his friend Sir Robert Walpole who lived at Houghton Hall. It takes the form of a wine cooler with exquisite carving around the side depicting a shipscape. A brightly painted memorial to the Green family, husband, wife, four sons and five daughters, dominates the south aisle. The faces must be portraits, they are so individual. Amongst the many ledgerstones in the church is one to Robinson Crusoe who died in 1773. Sad to relate there is no direct connection between him and the character in *Gulliver's Travels*, although it is possible he was named after the character who first appeared in 1726.

LITTLE WITCHINGHAM, ST FAITH

Completely isolated in a sylvan setting, this church is famed for its medieval wall paintings which were first discovered hidden under layers of limewash in 1967. Apart from these, it is a small, simple and stark church, which in many ways allows us to appreciate them even more. The floor is of local pamments and the roof timbers are limewashed in the traditional manner for a rural building. The paintings form two main series and date from the fourteenth century. In the nave are a series of scenes including St George and the dragon, the Harrowing of Hell, the Deposition and the Incredulity of St Thomas. Thanks to interpretation in the church they are easily recognised. In the south aisle are the most remarkable paintings, the symbols of the Four Evangelists in roundels, surrounded by trailing vines. Like most medieval wall paintings they have faded to a warm ochre, but here the details of the vines are amazingly preserved, and you can see the individual brush strokes on some of the leaves, which continue into the nave. There are few monuments in the church but a nicely cut ledgerstone records the burial of Thomas Outlaw in 1650. Outside the church, and often missed, is a remarkably well-preserved Crucifixion scene, carved into a piece of limestone, now set into the south chancel wall. In any other church this would be the main item of interest, but at Little Witchingham everything takes second place to the wall paintings.

MARSHAM, ALL SAINTS

Visible from the main road but approached via a farm track, this church is normally open only in the summer when it more than repays a special visit. With features dating from the thirteenth century onwards, this is one of those churches that never had a single donor wealthy enough to completely rebuild it and as a result it is something of a puzzle to identify the relevant dates. The main doorway to the south is thirteenth century in date and the door itself possibly only a hundred years later. It is covered with rusty iron nails, but only at face height, surviving from the display of official notices that have been posted on the door ever since. The plate behind the handle is medieval. Once inside we are confronted by a much larger church than the exterior would suggest. To the rear the font is one of the Seven Sacrament types with a high standard of carving, despite being damaged by iconoclasts. One of the least damaged scenes represents Marriage, and still retains a little of its original red colour. Sadly, the bride's head has completely gone but her husband is showing off his new haircut. The impressive roof is something of an amalgam. Originally it was of the hammerbeam type, but at some stage it was decided to replace the hammer beams with tie beams running across the width of the church. The diminutive angels retain their wings, which were, unusually, carved from the same piece of wood as their body. One of the arches of the south arcade has a fictive canopy painted on it, no doubt to give honour to a statue affixed to the pier beneath where, it will be noticed, the stringcourse has been cut back to allow for something tall. The rather insubstantial rood screen has lost its loft, but it is one of the most rewarding to study. The muntins are beautifully decorated with a vertical floral frieze whilst below are sixteen exceedingly well-executed saints. By comparing the backgrounds to the figures you will see that they were painted by two different artists. On the north side the backgrounds are alternately green and red, but on the south side the majority are green. Both sides have an attractive horizontal frieze at shoulder height, and throughout the figures have different poses which makes them more lifelike. Whilst some are easy to identify, for example St Peter and St John, others have no attributes to help us identify them. From medieval wills we know that the painting took place in the first decade of the fifteenth century. Visitors with binoculars will be able to see two rare survivals in stained glass: a tiny elephant and a unicorn high up in the north aisle. Another unicorn can be seen in the truly impressive royal arms painted on four planks of wood and displayed on the front of the organ gallery. It dates from the reign of King James I.

Hindringham. Now proved to be a late thirteenth-century chest. (Photo by John Vigar)

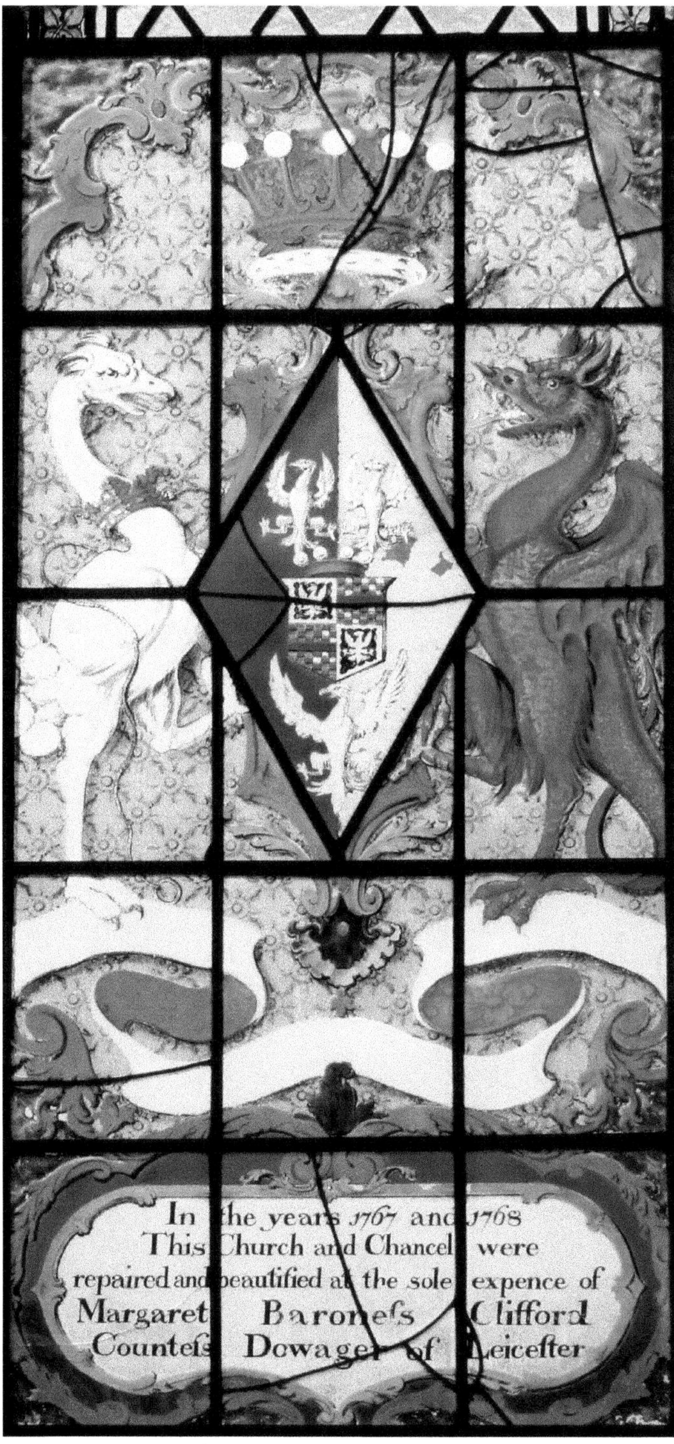

Holkham. Eighteenth-century heraldic glass. (Photo by John Vigar)

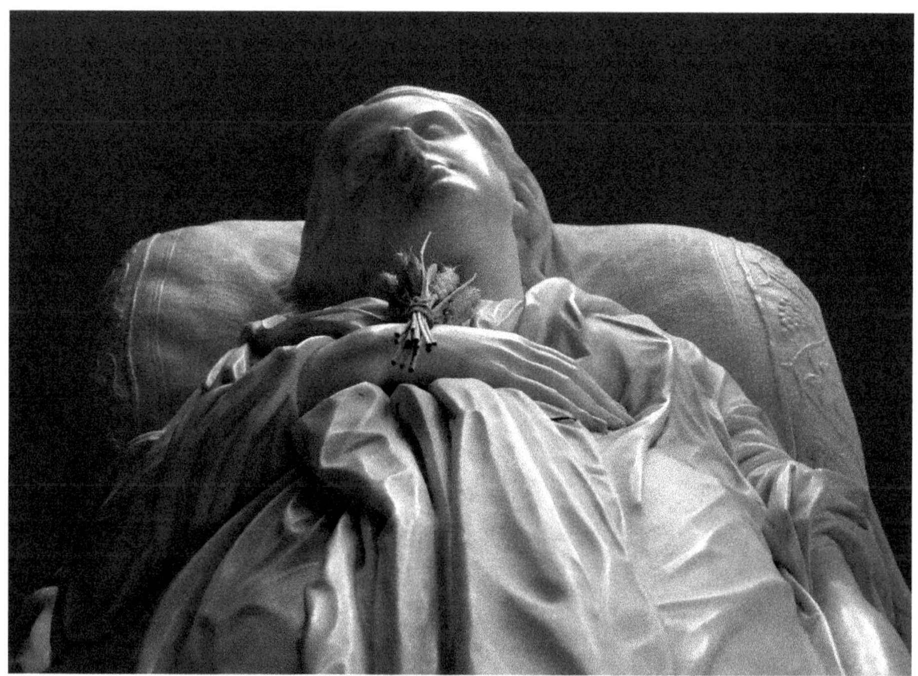

Holkham, Juliana, Countess of Leicester by Sir Joseph Boehm. (Photo by John Vigar)

King's Lynn, St Nicholas Chapel. Monument to Benjamin Keene 1757 designed by Robert Adam. (Photo by John Vigar)

King's Lynn, St Nicholas Chapel. West doors recently repainted in their original colours. (Photo by John Vigar)

Little Witchingham. Interior of the nave showing a series of medieval wall paintings. (Photo by John Vigar)

Above: Little Witchingham. Vine leaf and fruit wall paintings where every brush stroke can still be seen. (Photo by John Vigar)

Left: Marsham. This scene on the Seven Sacrament font depicts Matrimony. (Photo by John Vigar)

Norwich, St Giles

In a city of superlative medieval churches, it is difficult to choose just two for inclusion in this book, but St Giles on the Hill deserves to be better known. Its tower dominates the western end of the city and would originally have done so even more, before the construction of the Catholic cathedral. Medieval cities often had churches dedicated to St Giles, patron saint of lepers, close to a gateway, and this is no exception, standing just inside the city wall. From it the curfew bell still rings nightly, as it has done since the fifteenth century. Although the church had an extensive restoration in the nineteenth century, the interior is still characterful with a tall aisled nave flooded with light and an early hammerbeam roof. The chancel is entirely Victorian as the medieval chancel had been demolished in 1581. It is not surprising that an urban church like this is blessed with high-quality memorials, and two immediately catch the eye. In the south aisle is the memorial to Sir Thomas Churchman who died in 1781, signed by Thomas Rawlins who was the most accomplished Norwich mason of his day. Churchman was a weaver and mayor of the city and this display records his status for posterity. Below his shield of arms is a portrait bust of a well-fed man in curly wig. Beneath is a sarcophagus with very detailed symbolism showing the death of Time. Father Time lies dying on the ground whilst a cherub blows bubbles, symbolic of the short-lived nature of beautiful things. The figure on the right is Fame, pointing to the legend *Time Shall Be No More*. Nearby is the memorial to his father, a much more solid affair by the London sculptor Sir Henry Cheere, with three delightful winged cherubs by his signature at the base. The second memorial of note is in the north aisle and commemorates Dr William Offley who died in 1767. For the period it is disarmingly asymmetrical with an oval inscription supported by half a broken pediment and a stack of books whilst higher up is another half-broken pediment revealed by drapes. Whilst these monuments stand out others need to be searched for. One is a chalice brass of 1499 to the priest John Smyth. This belongs to a small number of the same type all made in Norwich around the year 1500, the inscription still being in Latin. The other is a brass to Elizabeth Bedingfield who died in 1633 and the inscription in English is rather sad and reminds us that all she has is 'A Bedding Field, A Peece of Earth, A Grave' and declaring that one day she will rise 'out of the earth and slime'. In pride of place in the nave is a medieval eagle lectern which has moved around the city from church to church, but which was first given in 1493, as shown on the dedicatory inscription that runs around the stem. The church is open at advertised times.

Norwich, St John Maddermarket

In the bustling pedestrian centre of the city, this church has been retired since 1981 and is open at set times. Small by Norwich standards, it nonetheless represents the civic history of the city through both its architecture and furnishings. From the street its long low façade is relieved only by the tall fifteenth-century tower, itself distinguished by a public right of way which cuts through its base via a vaulted passage. However, from the north the church looks far more impressive, seemingly dominating a hilltop position with a grand portal as befits a church which once squared up to the mansion of the Dukes of Norfolk. The clerestory is formed of limestone which is an elegant foil to the dark flint rubble construction of the rest of the church. Internally the church is much wider than it is long, because it lost its chancel during the late medieval period when city space was at a premium. The stonework of the current east window is fourteenth century, so must have been reused from the chancel when it was demolished. In the Lady Chapel is a rare painted ceiling showing the Sacred Monogram set into rosettes and fruity vines. Many churches must once have had such ceilings, but this is a rare survival. It is the memorials that one remembers at St John's. On the west wall is a series of memorial brasses collected from elsewhere in the church, interspersed with brass coffin plates, the typography of which display 300 years of design. The more eye-catching monuments are, of course, to families who owed their wealth to manufacturing industry, the Sothertons and Layers being depicted in brightly coloured alabaster tablets. A hundred years later the young Abigail Jenney (d. 1728) and her two children were commemorated by an architectural tablet footed by a pair of skulls. It was thc work of Augustine Curtis who signed his work with such a flourish it almost eclipses the inscription above. In the gallery is the finest tablet in the church, made of yellow marble and signed by Thomas Rawlins, who was himself a parishioner here. In the aisle is the ledgerstone he carved for his wife Mary where he is grandly described as an architect, but despite publishing a book of designs, he is predominantly remembered today as a monumental mason. The stained glass in St John's is especially rewarding. Fragments of high-quality Norwich glass is jumbled into a single window whilst there is a fine Tree of Jesse window by a later city glazier, King of Norwich 1916.

Ranworth, St Helen

This is justifiably one of the most visited churches in the county, popular among both hardened church crawlers and the more casual visitor in search of a picturesque church. Dominating its eponymous Broad, the tower is one of the few in Norfolk that is open to visitors, giving a unique perspective of this watery landscape, and welcoming sailors with its cosy café. The highlight of Ranworth is its ensemble of rood screen, cantor's desk and side chapels, forming the best surviving group of its type in England. The desk, being portable, is the most surprising survival. Whilst several Norfolk churches have their medieval lecterns, this one is different as it has the eagle symbol of St John the Evangelist painted on one side, whilst the other has a copy of the Gloria pasted onto it. When first made for the church it would have belonged in the chancel. The screen itself dates from the late fifteenth century and its lower panels are painted with the Twelve Apostles who, helpfully, bear their names below. There are eight further painted panels arranged to form a reredos to north and south altars, and these are a rather more unusual series of saints. The north side depicts St Etheldreda of Ely and St Barbara in its outer panels. The two central saints are not in their original form and have been overpainted. On the south side is an unusual representation of Our Lady squirting milk from her breast into the mouth of the Christ child. This is combined with St Margaret, St Mary Salome and St Mary Cleophas. Dividing the side altars from the screen are two parclose screens, each showing two more saints

Above: Norwich, St Giles. The church dominates the townscape. (Photo by Simon Knott)

Right: Norwich, St Giles. Donor inscription on the medieval lectern, 1493. (Photo by John Vigar)

and St George and St Michael respectively. The latter are the most famous images from Ranworth and certainly reward getting down onto your knees to examine them closely. In both paintings the intricate brush strokes are visible, the detail of St George's gauntlet being especially detailed, as is the blue dragon. St Michael's dragon has seven furious heads, which are being battered by his shield which has a most elaborate pommel. Miraculously Michael has fitted his sword in between his crown, halo and wings! At the back of the church is a rare antiphoner, or service book, in a glass case. Created in Norfolk, it is every bit as important as the panels on the screen in the detail of its craftsmanship. Lost after the Reformation, it was gifted to the church in the twentieth century.

Norwich, St Giles. The asymmetrical monument to William Offley, 1767. (Photo by Simon Knott)

Norwich, St John Maddermarket. Sotherton monument, 1608. (Photo by John Vigar)

Ranworth. This rare medieval service book is a true Norfolk treasure. (Photo by John Vigar)

Ranworth. The unique ensemble of screen, side altars and loft. (Photo by Simon Knott)

Ranworth. The outstanding image of St Michael the Archangel. (Photo by John Vigar)

RINGLAND, ST PETER

Too close to Norwich to register on many people's radar, St Peter's is an undiscovered church of great charm and interest. Set on the edge of a village green, first impressions are of a church that saw its peak of prosperity in the fifteenth century, although it had started life rather earlier. The chancel windows are typical of the fourteenth century, and the chancel walls retain much of their medieval plaster which would have hidden the rather patchy flint rubble construction. The tower, too, is fourteenth century, although its rather splendid parapet, together with the south porch and nave clerestory, is fifteenth. They are of knapped flint which is in great contrast to the rubble flint of a century earlier. The base of the porch in particular is very fine work with flushwork panels, some containing limestone shields on which would have been painted the arms of those who had contributed towards its erection. The south wall of the porch is completely faced with flushwork, although, unusually, it is also clearly coursed. Inside, the church is plastered in a sandy colour which gives it far more character than the sterile white so commonly used today. It ties in with the amazing roof, which is of familiar hammerbeam construction, but with the beams being hidden by coving which springs from the wall posts that run down between the clerestory windows. Angels rest on the coving just where they would spring from a traditional hammerbeam whilst carved corbels support the wall posts. Those on the east end, next to the chancel arch, are of three-quarter angels, giving honour to the rood that would have stood nearby. Beneath stands the base of the rood screen, the faces, hands and feet of its saints having sadly been removed by the iconoclasts, who obviously wanted to remove any reminders that the saints had once been ordinary people. Interestingly, each holds a ribbon text with the words each apostle is supposed to have added to what we now know as the Apostles' Creed, so we know exactly who these figures once represented. Although the writing is in Latin, some words are easy to pick out and it is at once obvious that they are in the wrong order and the creed cannot be read left to right, as it must have been planned. This is because the screen has had an eventful life and has been moved around the church before finally being placed back in its original position by someone who either couldn't read the words, or who didn't know their relevance. As only eight apostles now form the screen four have not made it back; three are missing completely and St Philip is still on his progress around the church and is now to be seen in the north aisle! All this fifteenth-century work would have been expensive and its donors would have wished us to remember them in our prayers – and it is here that Ringland church gives us a unique insight into the benefactors, for amongst other fragments of Norwich glass of the time are images and names of no fewer than seven of them! This reinforces our understanding that late work to churches was often a collaborative effort, rather than the gift of an individual. And so we must thank Matilde, Robert, John and others not only for this glass but also the other fifteenth-century additions to the church. Of great interest is a stained-glass roundel of a centaur, one of the best-preserved examples anywhere in England. It shows the creature with the head of a man but body of a horse playing a violin whilst out in the forest with his (very eager) dog. In the chancel the Ten Commandments frame the main altar whilst on the west wall, overlooking the East Anglian-type font, are two eighteenth-century hatchments of the Le Neve family.

SEDGEFORD, ST MARY

Located in the far north-west corner of Norfolk, and hidden off the main coast road, the village of Sedgeford hides its church on the side of a verdant valley. I suggest the visitor walks around the outside of the church first, because the view from the south is quite different to that from the north which prefaces a relatively simple church – but St Mary's is far from that! On the south we see that not only is it a round-towered church with aisles, but that it has an enormous south transept that encroaches on the chancel. The tower emerges from the west end of the nave and there are huge porches to both north and south aisles. Predominantly built of local flint, there are also patches of limestone used when it was available from boats along the coast. We step down into the church which must always have suffered from damp being at the base of a steep slope. The walls can be green with algae, although recent remedial works have been undertaken. The circular piers between nave and aisles are typically of the thirteenth century and look rather good beneath the much later clerestory windows, although one obviously failed and was replaced in the fourteenth century in the then up-to-date octagonal form. To complement the arcades there are a few remains of thirteenth-century wall paintings, especially the red-lined decoration to give the effect of blocks of stone. In this case some of the designs have elaborate flowers in them, complete with stalks which is an unusual addition. The font is the oldest thing to see here, of the usual late twelfth-century type with blank arcading around the square bowl. Next in date are the fragments of grey *grisaille* medieval glass now surrounded by yellowy-green clear panes. This design of glass was invented late in the twelfth century to fill complete windows, letting in as much light as possible without allowing worshippers to be distracted by things outside. Of the same date is the painted consecration cross visible on the aisle wall. This was added to the church when it was reopened following the construction of the aisles and would have been one of twelve in the church anointed with holy oil by the bishop. My favourite thing to see in Sedgeford is the veritable cornucopia of graffiti, ancient and modern. Crowded around the tower arch is an incomparable gallery of interesting incisions. One of the earliest is the undated compass-drawn design to catch evil spirits. As it goes over the thirteenth-century painting it must be slightly later. Easier to date are the initials carved by generations of Sedgefordians, some of them office holders like William Cram, parish clerk in 1665. These names are just crying out for some documentary research to be done on them! Other church treasures include the pokerwork chest with fretwork panels and the easily missed fifteenth-century stained-glass image of St Edward the Confessor holding his ring and a book, although his crowned head probably originally belonged to an entirely different figure!

SHELTON, ST MARY

Sir Ralph Shelton was one of the most prominent men in late fifteenth-century Norfolk. Together with the Paston, Boleyn and Bedingfield families, the Sheltons were prominent courtiers and servants of the royal houses of York and Tudor. Like most men of his period he was proud of his place in society and keen to ensure his memory outlived him. In 1497, just weeks before his death, he wrote his will in which he asked his executors to complete the rebuilding of Shelton church which he had already begun. Of the previous church the plain flint tower is the main survival. Ralph's new church is built of brick with stone dressings, seen to best advantage at the east end. Here a large three-light window of typical 'Tudor' design lights a sacristy behind the altar. These east end sacristies are a feature of Norfolk churches, especially of those dating from the end of the fifteenth century. To either side of the window are two elaborate image niches constructed of limestone, whilst above the window is a fork-bearded water spewer. The church may be built of brick, but it is not a utilitarian building, for it incorporates the black diaper patterns more familiar from Wolsey's Hampton Court Palace. The porch was obviously designed to house the priest in its upper room, but money was running out by the time it was built and the elaborate fan vaulting was started but never completed, allowing us to look from the ground at the blocked Tudor doorway and fireplace way above our heads. Inside, the church all is light and bright, and the huge clerestory windows together with the plastered ceiling create an upper greenhouse effect. No expense was spared in the planning of the church with a series of carved brackets running down each side of the nave which would originally have supported the wall posts of a hammerbeam roof. It might be argued that its removal in the eighteenth century improved the look of the church, even if it was a great historic loss. Shelton's rebus can be seen everywhere in the church, a barrel, or tun, and a shell, sometimes with his initial, an R. The rood screen has been cut down at dado height but the staircase that gave access to the loft is still open showing its height. After Shelton's death his wife wrote her will from which it is obvious that she had started to erect a tomb over her husband's grave. Unfortunately, after her death in 1500 money seems to have run out completely and the canopy over their tomb was never complete, leaving just the sides of the arch fitted with elaborately carved stone. Only the panels of the tomb chest itself were painted with the family shields of arms, as was a second tomb chest nearby in the north aisle. A century later the record for most elaborate monument in the church was taken by Sir Robert Houghton and his wife, for whom an extraordinary confection of statues, heraldry and *memento mori* was installed. High above the tower arch is an especially fine royal arms of King William III, which is one of the most elaborate in the county. In such a light church, stained glass is at a premium but there are some delightful details in the glass commissioned to commemorate Sir Ralph, as well as some continental glass of the same period.

South Creake, Our Lady St Mary

Our Lady St Mary is a large and characterful flint church set away from the through road that follows the River Burn as it flows northwards to the sea. The huge chancel, rebuilt by the patrons, Castle Acre Priory, dates from the thirteenth century but the main part of the church is a remodelling of a fourteenth-century structure. An unusual feature of the tower is that it includes image niches on its exterior, formed of the former putlog holes where wooden scaffolding formed part of the original structure. In many respects the interior of the church represents

Ringland. Here the hammerbeam roof is partly hidden by coving. (Photo by Matthew McDade)

how most medieval churches might once have looked. The absence of benches, uneven floors, splashes of colour from statues, and an abiding sense of being somewhere special make this a church unique in Norfolk. Surprisingly much of this character is the result of twentieth-century intervention, but the casual visitor probably doesn't need to know such detail. There is much to see. Firstly, the piers to north and south arcades stand on wide stone bases – a rare survival of medieval seating where the 'weak went to the wall'. Both arcades stop before the chancel arch. On the south side this allows room for the rood loft staircase, the upper door of which sits level with the top of the surviving screen. On the north side an unusual window has been cut through the wall. No doubt this somehow linked the altar on the north side of the screen and the altar in the north-east chapel, but exactly how it was used is open to debate. In the twentieth century a rood beam and figures was introduced, though at a slightly lower position than the original – look at the way the moulding around the arch above has been pared away to take the beam, the surviving corbels marking exactly where it once stood. The screen itself is original, as is the delightful wooden wine glass pulpit, one of just a handful in the county. It retains ghosts of its medieval paintwork, whilst on the chancel side of the screen you can see some interesting architectural graffiti including a delightful spired church. Unlike most Norfolk churches this screen has medieval doors. The nave roof is a splendid fifteenth-century hammerbeam construction with angels at the end of each beam joyfully painted in the twentieth century. On the west wall of the nave, above the tower arch is a tiny window, or hagioscope, which would have given the bell ringer a view into the church in order to ring the bell to mark the Consecration during the Mass. The south aisle roof is worth a

Ringland. Prominent flint flushwork panels top the west tower. (Photo by Simon Knott)

Above: Sedgeford.
A complex ground plan compared to most north Norfolk churches. (Photo by John Vigar)

Left: Shelton. The rebus of Richard Shelton showing his Shell and Barrel (Tun). (Photo by John Vigar)

Shelton. The striking brick exterior is a rare sight in Norfolk. (Photo by John Vigar)

South Creake. Interior looking east showing the fourteenth-century arcades. (Photo by John Salmon)

Shelton. This incomplete vault in the porch would have supported the priest's accommodation above. (Photo by John Vigar)

South Creake. The angels were repainted in the twentieth century. You can see the hagioscope window from the tower into the nave. (Photo by John Vigar)

close inspection as its spandrels are carved with a series of animals taken straight from a medieval bestiary including a cockatrice and a unicorn. On the floor under the parish bier is the oldest feature in the church: a thirteenth-century stone coffin lid with the familiar double-omega symbol showing that it was probably made at Barnack near Peterborough. For lovers of stained glass this church contains some excellent pieces as there are both jumbles of medieval fragments and some high-quality continental glass panels.

South Lopham, St Andrew

Most Norfolk churches are representative of the late medieval period when the county was at its most wealthy and pious. We will never know just how much earlier work was lost at that time of wholesale rebuilding and replacement, but at South Lopham stands one of the few churches to have retained its earlier form. And what form! St Andrew's is a Romanesque church of the twelfth century which has a linear plan of nave, central tower and chancel. Whilst we are more familiar with central towers that make cruciform churches, a surprisingly large number were not conceived as anything other than a linear plan. The tower here is fortress-like in its simplicity with blank arcading carried over its upper three levels. Only the flint flushwork parapet speaks of a later period, as does the south aisle of the church with its flushwork initials between each window. Inside, the nave seems extremely tall, a feeling accentuated by the fact that there is no north aisle, and this leads us to an important discovery – that much of the north wall predates the tower and is Saxon. This is proven by the circular window near the west end which is typical of the period and which was formed purely by flints being built around a wicker basket which was then removed. In contrast, the Normans always used dressed stone as the edges of their windows. The fantastic Norman arches between nave, tower and chancel exude an air of solidity, whilst the nave roof does the opposite in its fifteenth-century attempt to mimic a hammerbeam roof without bringing the weight onto the hammerbeam itself, making it a false hammerbeam roof. Many churches used this design successfully, but it doesn't really work against the massive Norman arch. Again, in contrast, is the entirely fourteenth-century chancel, rebuilt after the Black Death by the rector, Nicholas de Horton. There are many fine bench ends throughout the church. One shows an elephant with a howdah on its back, but the carver had probably only seen an illustration of an elephant and gave it both hooves and a beak! Another shows a blacksmith with anvil, whilst my favourite depicts a cat with a massive rabbit in its mouth.

Thompson, St Martin

Here is a true church crawler's church, with lots of interesting details that collectively give us a church that is worth a long journey to see. Our story really starts in 1349 when this church was made a Collegiate Foundation with a college of priests endowed to pray for the souls of its dead benefactors, Thomas and John de Shardelow. The building the priests lived in survives as College Farmhouse a short distance away. Always a small foundation, the constant journeys from home to church by the priests must have been a familiar sight until it closed in 1547. The structure of the church altered very little from the date of its foundation until the addition of the present rood screen and a south nave chapel in the fifteenth century. Today the church draws thousands of visitors each year keen to see the patina of its furnishings, untouched by nineteenth-century restorers. The font is contemporary with the Foundation and has cusped panels on its eight sides, showing that this remained a parish church and was not just reserved for prayers for the dead. The nave is fitted with benches with *fleur de lys* ends, a true example of *Gothic survival*, bearing the surprisingly late dates of 1625 and 1632, but there is also a family pew in the more usual classical form popular at the time with knobbed finials. The pulpit, too, is early seventeenth century with backplate and sounding board. The screen dates from the mid-fourteenth century with the most delicious tracery based on cusped wheels and, unusually, with contemporary doors painted green and red. The base of the screen has some exciting medieval paintwork too, in an elaborate *fleur de lys* pattern, rather than the more traditional images of saints. The chancel contains stalls for the College of Priests, and some have misericord seats. It seems that the stalls were originally 'return' seats as the painted design on the eastern face of the screen doesn't continue below the top third, suggesting that seats facing the altar originally sat there, which makes the current stalls a few generations later. The chancel roof was rebuilt in the seventeenth century and the date 1648 and the initials RF can be clearly seen. Many windows in the chancel are either completely or partially blocked, no doubt done at a time when it was cheaper to repair a broken window this way rather than to reglaze it. The sedilia in the chancel is one of the most splendid in Norfolk and dates from the fourteenth century. It comprises three seats and a piscina all within a horizontal-headed frame, in the spandrels of which are three green men with foliage coming out of their mouths. Amongst other items of interest are two medieval chests, consecration crosses, a tablet to a London dealer in horn and another to Prince Frederick Duleep Singh (d. 1936), a great supporter of historic Norfolk churches who saved this church from closure in 1913.

THURNING, ST ANDREW

Viewed from the gate, this church seems rather plain. The severe west tower and nave with just three small south windows are not what we have come to expect from a Norfolk church. There is not even a chancel at the east end as this was demolished as surplus to requirements in the eighteenth century, leaving a few fragments standing. However, the interior is a gem, full of box pews and other furniture originally made in the eighteenth century for Corpus Christie College, Cambridge, and moved here in 1825. St Andrew's is one of the churches in their patronage. It is clear, even from a cursory glance, that these are of a much higher quality than is normally found in Norfolk at that date. The rounded 'corners' by the tower are especially well done, as are the slightly tapering legs of the seats in the boxes. These pews would have been rented by the wealthy families for themselves and their servants. The open benches in the nave would have been for the poor who could not have afforded rent. In the 1851 Census of Religious Worship we find that there were 100 free seats and 150 rented seats, bringing in £300 a year. Average attendance at Sunday services, including children, was 100 in the morning and 145 in the afternoon, which wasn't bad for a population of 200. The pulpit and the three-sided altar rails came in at the same time as the box pews. The church contains many memorials to the Elwin, Wake and Gay families. Most notable is that to Elizabeth and William Wake (he died 1750 on the way back from Bombay where he had served eight years as Governor). The coloured marble at the bottom is of the highest quality. Nearby is the architecturally perfect memorial to Caleb Elwin (d. 1776) designed by Edward Holl of Norwich. If you can, visit Thurning to see the snowdrops in the churchyard.

TRUNCH, ST BOTOLPH

Standing in a part of Norfolk where every church could make a claim for inclusion in this book, St Botolph swings it by offering something rare in the county: a free-standing font cover. It was built to give honour to the sacrament of baptism and allows the funeral party to stand completely under its canopy – a sixteenth-century gazebo if you like. It is covered with miniscule carvings and was originally covered with paint as well and would also have had free-standing statuary. Still visible is a painted Crucifixion facing down the gangway towards the altar.

You could spend hours looking at the details of carving. I especially like the pig with crozier, a woodpecker and a dormouse with its nuts – you must search them out in the jungle of vines, leaves, flowers and fruit. The canopy itself has a vault which contains a circlet of *fleur de lys*. The rest of the church has much to offer. Some Norwich glass survives high up depicting musical angels, whilst the screen retains its twelve painted apostles. There is also a ribbon inscription asking for prayers for the souls of the donors, but sadly they are unnamed. My friend Simon Knott (www.norfolkchurches.co.uk) points out that there is a consecration cross on the north side of the screen doorway, showing that screen and church are contemporary. In two of the panels the brocade background has been painted in three dimensions, to look like a screen, and behind is a lovely blue sky with fluffy clouds and a bizarre shower of flowers! The alternating red and green backgrounds of the other panels on the screen have been cleverly reproduced in the nineteenth-century reredos. The return stalls are set on acoustic jars to amplify medieval voices, the northern two sound openings having very elaborately carved traceried openings, whilst the stalls themselves are covered in graffiti. Look for the elaborate tower (which might be a lighthouse) and the windmill with four be-sailed arms. In the nave the hammerbeam roof has carved spandrels of a variety of designs whilst outside, the priest's door has a little porch of its own rather unfortunately set underneath a clasping buttress. Good engineering it is not, but a delightful composition, nonetheless.

South Lopham. This grand Norman central tower is distinguished by blank arcading. (Photo by Simon Knott)

South Lopham. An elephant bench end carved by someone who had probably only ever heard of one. (Photo by Simon Knott)

Thompson. Consecration cross incised and painted on the wall to mark the place anointed by the Bishop when the church was consecrated. (Photo by John Vigar)

Thompson. A fourteenth-century collegiate church. (Photo by John Vigar)

Thompson. One of the most atmospheric churches in the county. On the left you can see the staircase to the Rood Loft, and south chapel to the right. (Photo by John Vigar)

Trunch. The font canopy retains a large amount of original paint on its upper surfaces. (Photo by Simon Knott)

Trunch. This wooden canopy totally encloses the font beneath it. (Photo Simon Knott)

Upper Sheringham. Interior looking east towards the original rood screen and its surviving loft. (Photo by John Vigar)

Upper Sheringham. One of several fantastical bench ends. (Photo by John Vigar)

Upper Sheringham, All Saints

Until the growth of holiday resorts this *was* Sheringham, a medieval agricultural village on the north-facing slopes overlooking the North Sea. In the nineteenth century it quickly became eclipsed by the new settlement that by then had its own church, and today Upper Sheringham is a delightful little-visited backwater. That the country was more important than the sea to this area during the Middle Ages may be seen from the south porch with its flushwork, pinnacles and armorial spandrels. In comparison the main entrance today, from the north, is totally without pretension. The church is a fifteenth-century rebuild with few references to earlier structures other than the tower and clerestory windows. The font stands on high steps with each of its side panels displaying a different design of window tracery. However, it is the woodwork that brings us to this lovely light church. The rood screen is typical of the fifteenth century, but what makes this church unique in East Anglia is the fact that its loft was not destroyed at the Reformation. It is supported on wooden braces which are set into the easternmost piers of the north and south arcades. These are both carved with a fantastic beast in the spandrels. That on the south side is just how we expect a dragon to look, but its counterpart on the north side is a combination of lion and a pelican. This may represent a form of Griffin – a land-based creature with wings who could be seen to represent Christ who linked Earth and Heaven. Other woodwork of interest includes bench ends depicting a mermaid, a cat with a kitten and a chrism baby wrapped in swaddling. Above the font is a carved beam that would once have held a counterbalanced font cover.

Walpole St Peter, St Peter

In the wide-open Fenland, famed for its medieval wealth, St Peter's Church is the embodiment of that wealth displayed in stone to the Glory of God, and nothing in the landscape can prepare the visitor for the grandeur of this magnificent building. The present building started life as a rebuild of an earlier church that had been destroyed in a flood of 1330. No sooner had rebuilding commenced than England was hit by the Black Death of 1348, so work towards its completion was slow. However, the plague had also focussed the mind and rebuilding might be seen as a way to thank God for survival and to pray that men's misdeeds would not incur God's wrath again. In many ways it is a church of dates, for records and visible evidence have left us with a calendar with which to work out the progress of rebuilding. We enter through the south porch with its gallery of carved bosses, dateable to a bequest from John Goddard of 1435. The font is dated 1532, the poor box 1639, the pulpit 1620, and gates to the south chapel 1708. There were bequests to the chancel windows in 1425. However helpful these dates are, they don't convey the unique atmosphere of St Peter's Church, and every visitor will find the individual detail that 'makes' the church for them. For some it will be the Hudd, or Parsons' churchyard shelter, for others the rare processional passage under the chancel which allowed processions to circumnavigate the church. For me it is the stone carving in the chancel where a series of blank arcades with fictive vaulting lines the walls. Hidden amongst the carvings are a series of tiny faces – some singing, some grimacing and others of monsters. In contrast, larger figures dominate the tower arch who I always refer as 'Mr Beard Tickler and his wife'. How I wish we knew who they were!

WICKHAMPTON, ST ANDREW

Overlooking the marshes that fringe the Broads, this is an undiscovered church with much of interest, especially as it did not get the typical Norfolk makeover in the fifteenth century. The earliest part of the church is the Norman chancel, rebuilt in the thirteenth century, probably by the Gerbygge family whose magnificent tombs line the north wall. The nave and tower are slightly later. We enter through the south door with magnificent medieval door furniture, contemporary with the nave. Immediately we see the amazing series of wall paintings that run along the north wall. They include an exceptional representation of the Three Living and Three Dead which is almost complete along with trees that are obviously bending in the wind. The Seven Acts of Mercy panel is well worth looking at in detail, especially for the fourteenth-century costume portrayed. As we enter the chancel the tombs of William Gerbygge and his wife dominate. They date from the thirteenth century, although the elaborate cusped canopies were recut in the nineteenth century. Sir William holds a heart – offering it up to Heaven, whilst his wife is devoutly in prayer, the relative simplicity of their clothes in contrast to the later wall paintings. Battered they may be, but to my mind they represent the very best of a period so infrequently found in the county.

WIGGENHALL MAGDALENE, ST MARY MAGDALENE

The four surviving medieval churches in the Wiggenhall villages are all worth visiting, but Magdalene is the one to visit for an all-round experience. It stands like a well-dressed elephant surrounded by low-level housing on the edge of the River Great Ouse. Built of carstone, limestone and brick, its external highlight is the pair of turrets at the junction of nave and chancel which take stairs up to the rood screen and onto the roof leads. Internally, the view from west to east shows a very prominent lean to the chancel – a result of a medieval rebuild relying on a different easterly orientation. The doors to the rood loft to either side of the chancel arch are extremely high up, showing that the loft was not part of the screen, as is more usually the case. The nave roof has a series of delightful carvings representing musicians, angels and at least one bishop. In the north aisle is a series of stained-glass images of saints popular in the fifteenth century but little known today including St Sampson, St Callistus, St Leger and St Lambert. Helpfully many are named (take binoculars). At the west end of the church are panels from the rood screen, one, St Mark's lion, poking its tongue out. Nearby is a domed chest of the type imported into the eastern counties from Danzig in the fifteenth century, and the church retains its fine decalogue, a board recording the Ten Commandments.

Walpole St Peter. A seventeenth-century poor box dated 1639. (Photo by John Vigar)

Walpole St Peter. Underneath the chancel is a passage to allow processions to go around the church without leaving the churchyard. (Photo by Simon Knott)

Walpole St Peter. A singing face hidden in the elaborate chancel wall arcading. (Photo by John Vigar)

Wickhampton. Exterior from the south-east. The window on the right is thirteenth century, those on the left a hundred years later. (Photo by John Vigar)

Wickhampton. The effigy of William Gerbygge, thirteenth century, is shown offering his heart to Heaven.

Wickhampton. A detail of the Seven Acts of Mercy showing the burial of the dead in a fourteenth-century wall painting. (Photo by John Vigar)

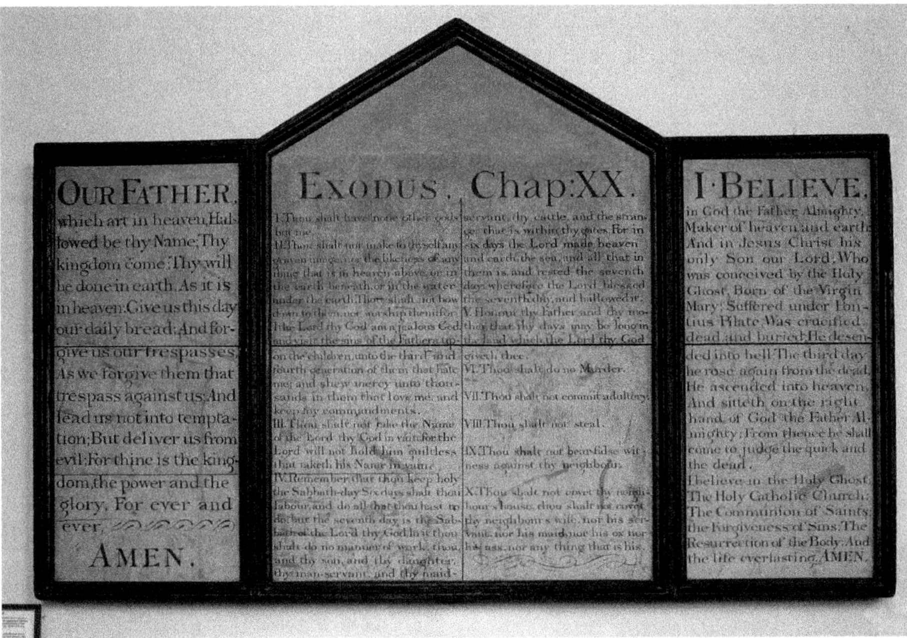

Wiggenhall, St Mary Magdalene. The Ten Commandments painted on boards. (Photo by Simon Knott)

Above: Wiggenhall, St Mary Magdalene. Exterior showing the enormous range of building materials including carstone, brick and limestone. (Photo by John Vigar)

Left: Wiggenhall, St Mary Magdalene. This angel in the roof would originally have held a thurible in the raised hand. (Photo by John Vigar)

CW00641051

LIVES
of the
NORTHUMBRIAN
SAINTS

LIVES
of the
NORTHUMBRIAN
SAINTS

By

S BARING-GOULD

Selected reprints from the author's sixteen-volume work 'LIVES OF THE SAINTS.'
ISBN 0947992 40 5
LLANERCH ENTERPRISES, 1990.

CONTENTS

S. OSWALD, K.M.

(A.D. 642).

[Sarum and York Kalendars, Anglican Martyrologies, Scottish Kalendars, Roman Martyrology, in the Belgian Kalendars, June 20, F. of Translation to Winnochberg,—German Breviaries and Missals of the 15th and 16th cent. Authority :—Bede's Anglo-Saxon Hist. The following life is for the most part condensed from that by Montalembert, in his "Monks of the West."]

THE conversion of Ethelbert of Kent, by Augustine, produced little or no effect on the North of England. Northumbria remained heathen ; Paulinus, who had borne the cross into Yorkshire, had preached at Dewsbury, and baptized at Catterick, had deserted the scene of his labours, and invasion and havoc had swept over it, obliterating his traces. It was not to S. Augustine and Ethelbert, but to SS. Aidan and Oswald that Northumbria was to look as its apostles. The father of the Christianity of the vast region now included in the counties of Yorkshire, Durham, and Northumberland, was not S. Gregory, but S. Columba, its metropolis was not Canterbury, but Iona.

Forty-eight years after Augustine and his Roman monks had landed on the shores of pagan England, an Anglo-Saxon prince invoked the aid of the monks of Iona, the children of Columba, for the conversion for the Saxons of the North. Augustine had bitterly upbraided the Celtic Church of Britain with doing nothing to convert the Saxons to Christ. That Church was now about nobly to repel that charge, by working a transformation in the North equal to that wrought in the South by the missionaries of Rome.

That Anglo-Saxon prince was Oswald, son of Ethelfrid the Ravager, and of the sister of the martyred King Edwin. After the defeat and death of his father, the son of the great enemy and conqueror of the Scots had, while yet a child, sought a refuge, along with his brother and a numerous train of young nobles, among the Scots.

In exile he spent the seventeen years of the reign of his uncle Edwin, as Edwin himself had lived in exile during the reign of his brother-in-law and persecutor Ethelfrid. But between these two representatives of the two dynasties which divided Northumberland, and succeeded each other in the sovereignty, there was this difference, that the young Edwin had sought and found an asylum among his pagan fellow-countrymen; while the banishment of Oswald led him into intercourse with people of a race and religion differing from his own.

Since the apostolate of Columba, the Scots and Picts had become entirely Christian, and among them Oswald and his companions in misfortune learned the truths of Christianity, and were all baptized, according to the rite of the Celtic Church, which differed from the Roman.

After the overthrow of Edwin, and the Deïrian dynasty,

the princes of the Bernician family returned to Northumbria, from which they had been banished for seventeen years.[1]

The elder, Eanfrid, fell by the sword of the Briton Cadwallon, after having renounced the Christian faith. But his younger brother Oswald was a man of very different stamp. At the head of a small but resolute band, of whom a dozen at most were Christians, like himself, he undertook to reconquer his country, and did not hesitate to carry on the struggle against the immense forces of the formidable Briton, nor even to attack him in pitched battle.

The two armies, so unequal in numbers, met near that great wall which the Emperor Severus had erected from sea to sea to keep back the Picts, and which divided Northumbria into two nearly equal parts. This rampart, which had neither restrained the Picts in their invasions of the South, nor the Saxons in their conquests to the North, was then, though not intact, still standing; as indeed even now its vast remains may be traced on the steep hill-tops and uplands, covered with heath or strewn with basalt rocks, which give to that district of England an aspect so different from that of her ordinary landscapes. Flanked by a fragment of the Roman wall, the Anglo-Saxon prince occupied a height where his feeble forces could defy the attack of the numerous battalions of Cadwallon. On that height, which was afterwards called *Heaven's Field*, and which still bears the name of S. Oswald, on the eve of the day of decisive battle, the young and ardent warrior held erect with his own

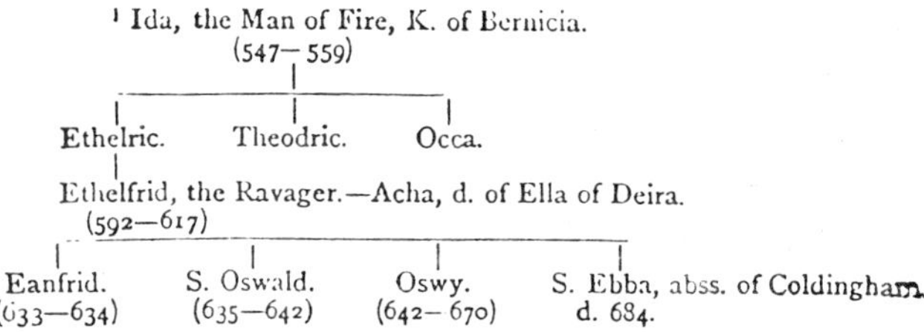

hands a large wooden cross, which had been hastily made by his orders, while his companions heaped the earth round it, to keep it firm in its position; then, prostrating himself before it, he said to his brothers in arms, "Let us all fall on our knees, and together implore the living and true and Almighty God in His mercy to defend us against the pride and fierceness of our enemy; for that God knows our cause is just, and that we fight for the salvation of our nation. Yes, it is for our salvation and our freedom that we might fight to-day against those Britons, whom our fathers gloried in challenging, but who now prophesy the extirpation of our race."

The Britons themselves might seem to have an equal right to offer this prayer, for they had long been Christians, and after all had only retaken their native soil from the grasp of foreign invaders. But a century of possession had given the latter a conviction of their right; and the bloody cruelties of Cadwallon had dishonoured his patriotism. Oswald, moreover, represented the cause of advancing Christianity; for the Britons did nothing to convert their enemies, and the cross which he planted was the first which had been as yet seen in Bernicia.

On the evening of the same day, and during the night which preceded the contest which was to fix his destiny, Oswald, asleep in his tent, saw in a dream the holy S. Columba, the apostle and patron of the country of his exile, and of the church in which he had received his baptism. The warlike Abbot of Iona, who had been dead for thirty-six years, appeared to him shining with angelic beauty; erect, and with that lofty stature that distinguished him in life, he stood and stretched his resplendent robe over the whole of the small army of exiles as if to protect it; then, addressing the prince, he said, as God said to Joshua before the passage of the Jordan, "Be of good courage, and play the man. At the break of day march to the battle: I have obtained for thee from God the victory over thine enemies and the death of tyrants: thou shalt conquer and reign." The prince, on awaking, told his vision to the Saxons who had joined him, and all promised to receive baptism, like himself and the twelve companions of his exile, if he should return a conqueror. Early on the morrow the battle began, and Oswald gained a victory as complete as it was unlikely. Cadwallon, the last hero of the British race--victor, according to the Welsh tradition, in forty battles and in sixty single combats—perished in this defeat. The Britons evacuated Northumbria, never to return, and withdrew behind the Severn. Those who remained to the north of the Dee, in the territory which has since been divided into the counties of Chester, Lancaster, and Westmoreland, submitted to the Northumbrian sway, which henceforth extended from the Irish Channel to the North Sea, tracing the line of the east coast as far as Edinburgh. There still remained, however, out of Wales, and to the south of the wall of Severus, in the region adjoining Caledonia, a district bathed by the waters of the Solway, full of lakes and hills like Caledonia itself, and then, as now, known by the name of Cumbria or Cumberland, where the Britons continued independent, relying on the support of the Scots, and in alliance with the people of their own race who dwelt on the banks of the Clyde. But they fell, and, though subdued, agreed in bestowing upon the son of the Ravager—the great-grandson of the Burner—the Saxon who had nobly vanquished them, the name of *Lamn-Garm;* which means, according to some, "the Shining Sword," according to others, "the Liberal Hand."

Nothing is known of the course of events which, after the defeat and death of the great British chief, confirmed Oswald in the undisputed sovereignty of the whole of Northumbria and the temporal supremacy of the entire

Saxon Heptarchy; but we find him entitled Emperor of all Britain, by a writer almost contemporary with himself. Not only, says Bede, had he learned to possess in hope the heavenly kingdom which his forefathers knew not; but in this world God gave him a kingdom vaster than that possessed by any of his ancestors. He reigned over the four races who shared Britain among them—the Britons, the Scots, the Picts, and the Angles. No doubt this supremacy was but partially acknowledged, especially beyond the limits of the Anglo-Saxon territory; but Northumbria, when united under one king, could not fail to become at once the chief power of the Confederation. Oswald, who was the great-grandson of Ina on his father's side, and grandson of Ella on his mother's, had a natural right to unite the two realms of Deira and Bernicia, while at the same time delivering them from the humiliating and bloody yoke of the Britons and Mercians. He seems to have had a special affection for Bernicia, his father's country, in which he lived, and whose ancient boundaries on the Caledonian side he extended or re-established. But he succeeded, we are told by the Northumbrian Bede, in reconciling and binding into one State the two tribes which, although of the same race, had lived in continual conflict. He made of the two a real nation.

Oswald was the sixth of the great chiefs or suzerains of the confederation who bore the title of *Bretwalda*, before whom was carried the *tufa*, or tuft of feathers, which was the emblem of supreme authority, and which, after this, was used by none save by the Northumbrian kings. It is supposed that this dignity was conferred or ratified by the suffrage, not only of all the kings of the Heptarchy, but also of the principal chiefs or barons of each tribe. It was at first exclusively military; but it became under Oswald and his successors, as it had already been with Ethelbert of

Kent, a means of exercising great influence in religious matters. For Oswald was not only a true king and a gallant soldier, but also a good Christian, destined to become a saint; and in the power with which he found himself invested he saw chiefly the means of defending and propagating the faith which he had received with his baptism from the hands of the sons of Columba.

As soon as Oswald was established on his father's throne, his first and dearest thought was to bring back and to procure the triumph in his own country of that religion which had been the consolation of his exile. For this end missionaries, ministers of the Word of God, were necessary above all things. It did not occur to him to seek them in the church of Canterbury, the monastic centre which already existed on English soil, and whence ten years before had come Paulinus, the first Apostle of Northumbria. He does not seem to have even thought of the noble and worthy Roman deacon, James, whom Paulinus, on abandoning his metropolitan see of York, had left alone behind him; and who, remaining gallantly at his post during the storm of invasion and havoc, had continued to baptize and preach, and to snatch his prey from the old enemy. This deacon, however, was the lieutenant of a bishop to some extent identified with the Deïrian dynasty, and with the family of King Edwin, which had exiled, robbed, and supplanted the family of Oswald, and which he had just supplanted in his turn. Was it for this reason, as has been supposed, that Oswald sought no aid from the Roman missionaries? Is it not more natural to conclude that he was chiefly influenced by his remembrance of the generous hospitality which he had found among the Scots, and of the instructions of those from whom in early manhood he received baptism and the other Sacraments of the Church? Be this as it may, it was to the Scottish Church that he addressed himself—that is to say, to the heads of monasteries ruled by the traditions and institutions of Columba, that great Abbot of Iona who appeared to him in his dream the night before the decisive battle, to promise him victory and a crown.

Under the influence of that Celtic patriotism which inflamed the Britons against the conquering strangers, and which was no less unwilling to concede to them a share in eternal salvation than in the British soil, the Scottish or Irish Church seems, up to this time, to have refrained from all effort to spread the Gospel among the Saxons. But the time had come to adopt a different course. As though it had only awaited the signal given by Oswald, the Celtic Church, aided by the brave missionaries who sprang from that monastic reformation of which Iona was the centre, immediately began to light up with its radiance the whole northern region of Saxon Britain, from whence it went on into the territory where it had been preceded by the Roman missionaries, and where the two apostolic agencies finally met. The appeal of Oswald to Iona was responded to with apostolic warmth and eagerness for the work of winning souls to Christ. The gentle Aidan, whose memory should be dear to all Northumbrians, was sent from the monastic metropolis of Iona to found the Church on the land north of the Humber.

The story of his labours will be told elsewhere.[1] The king and the bishop rivalled each other in virtue, in piety, in ardent charity, and desire for the conversion of souls. Thanks to their mutual and unwearied efforts, every day saw the Christian religion spreading further and taking deeper root; every day joyous crowds hastened to feed on the bread of the Divine Word, and to plunge into the waters of baptism; every day numerous churches, flanked by monasteries and schools, rose from the soil. Every day new gifts

[1] Aug. 31.

of land, due to the generosity of Oswald and the Northumbrian nobles, came to swell the patrimony of the monks and the poor. Every day also new missionaries, full of zeal and fervour, arrived from Ireland or Scotland to help on the work of Aidan and Oswald, preaching and baptizing converts. And, at the same time, James the Deacon, sole survivor of the former Roman mission, redoubled his efforts to help forward the regeneration of the country in which he had already seen the Faith flourish and decay.

Oswald did not content himself with giving his friend Aidan the obedience of a son, and the support of a king, in all that could aid in the extension and consolidation of Christianity. He himself gave a perfect example of all the Christian virtues, and often passed whole nights in prayer, still more occupied with the concerns of the heavenly kingdom than with those of the earthly realm which he had so ably won, and for which he was so soon to die. He was not only lavish in alms, giving of his riches with humble and tender charity, to the humble and the poor, to the sick, to travellers, and to needy strangers who came to the bishop to be nourished with the word of life. In addition he constituted himself Aidan's interpreter, "and it was," says Bede, "a touching spectacle to see the king, who had, during his long exile, thoroughly learned the Celtic tongue, translating to the great chiefs and the principal officials of his court, the lords and thanes, the sermons of the bishop, who, as yet, spoke but imperfectly the language of the Anglo-Saxons.

The tender friendship and apostolic brotherhood which thus united the king and the bishop of the Northumbrians has, perhaps, more than anything else, contributed to exalt and hallow their memory in the annals of Catholic England.

Oswald was too active, too popular, too energetic, and too powerful not to make his actions and influence felt beyond the bounds of his own kingdom. Oswald contributed largely to the conversion of the most powerful kingdom of the Heptarchy, next to Northumbria—that of the Saxons of the west,—Wessex, a kingdom which was destined to absorb and supplant all the others. The kings of this nation also professed to be of the blood of Odin; they were descended from a chief called Cerdic, perhaps the bravest of all the invaders of the British soil, and who had consolidated his conquest by forty years of craft and war. It was among this warlike race that Oswald sought a wife; but contrary to ordinary precedent, it was, in this new union, the husband and not the wife, who took the initiative in conversion. When he went for his bride, Kineburga, into the country of the West Saxons, the King of Northumbria met there an Italian bishop, who had undertaken their conversion, finding them entirely pagan. He did his best to second the laborious efforts of the foreign missionary, and the king, whose daughter he was about to wed, having consented to be baptized, Oswald stood sponsor for him, and thus became the spiritual father of him whose son-in-law he was about to become. He took back to Northumbria with him the young convert who soon bore him a son, little worthy of his sire, but yet destined at least to be the founder of a monastery which acted a part of some importance in the history of the people.

All this prosperity was soon to end, as all that is good and beautiful ends here below. The terrible Penda was still alive, and under the iron hand of that redoubtable warrior, Mercia remained the stronghold of paganism, even as Northumbria had become under Edwin and Oswald the centre of Christian life in Great Britain. He had left unrevenged the death of his ally, the Briton, Cadwallon; he had done nothing to hinder the accession and establishment of a new Christian king in Northumbria. But when that king essayed to cross the river which formed the boundary of the two kingdoms, and to unite to his domain a province which had always belonged to the Mercians, Penda, notwithstanding his age, resumed his old inveteracy towards those whom he saw—again like Edwin—deserting the worship of their common ancestor Odin, and claiming an insupportable supremacy over all the Saxons, Pagan or Christian. He accordingly renewed with the Britons the alliance which had already been so disastrous to the Northumbrians, and, placing himself at the head of the two combined armies, waged for two years a sanguinary war against Oswald, which ended in a decisive battle at Maserfeld, on the western border of Mercia and Northumbria. The struggle was fierce; the brother of Penda perished in the fight, but Oswald, the great and beloved Oswald, shared the same fate. He died on the field, in the flower of his years, at the age of thirty-eight. There he fell—the historian of the English Church says, with emphasis—fighting for his country. But his last word, his last thought, was for heaven, and for the eternal welfare of his people. "My God," said he, on seeing himself encircled with enemies, overwhelmed by numbers, and already pierced by a forest of arrows and lances—"My God! save their souls." The last cry of this saintly spirit, this young hero, remained long graven on the memory of the Saxon people, and passed into a proverb to denote those who prayed without ceasing in life and in death.

The ferocity of Penda was not even satisfied by the death of his young rival. When the dead body of the King of Northumbria was brought from the battle-field into his presence, the old savage caused the head and hands of the hero to be cut off, and set up on stakes, to intimidate both conquerors and conquered. The noble remains were thus exposed for a whole year, till his brother and avenger, Oswy, carried them away. The hero's head was then taken to Lindisfarne, to the great monastery which he had so richly endowed, and where his holy friend Aidan awaited it; but his hands were deposited in a chapel in the royal fortress of Bamborough, the cradle of that Northumbrian dominion which the arms of his ancestors had founded, and which his own had so valiantly restored.

Thus perished, at the age of thirty-eight, Oswald, ranked by the Church among her martyrs, and by the Anglo-Saxon people among its saints and heroes of most enduring fame. Through the obscurity of that thankless and confused age, the eye rests gratefully on this young prince, reared in exile among the hereditary enemies of his race, who was consoled for the loss of a throne by his conversion to Christianity, who regained the kingdom of his fathers at the point of the sword, and planted the first cross on his native soil at the moment when he freed it from the usurper, crowned by the love and devotion of the people on whom he bestowed the blessings of peace and of supreme truth, spending his very life for its sake; united for a few short years to a wife whom, in marrying, he had made a Christian; gentle and strong, serious and sincere, pious and intelligent, humble and bold, active and gracious, a soldier and a missionary, a king and a martyr, slain in the flower of his age on the field of battle, fighting for his country, and praying for his subjects. Where shall we find in all history a hero more nearly approaching the ideal, more richly gifted, more worthy of eternal remembrance, and, it must be added, more completely forgotten?

S. AIDAN, B. OF LINDISFARNE.

(A.D. 651.)

[Roman Martyrology. York Kalendar, Bede, Ado, Usuardus, Aberdeen Breviary. Donegal and other Irish Kalendars. Authority:—Bede in his Eccl. History of England.[1]]

WHEN S. Oswald sought to convert his kingdom of Northumbria to Christ, as has been already related in his life, he turned to Iona for a missionary.

The Scottish monks answered his appeal with heartiness. But the first effect of their zeal was not fortunate. Their first representative seems to have been a man of harsh, unbending disposition, of that tone of mind prone to look on the gloomy side of affairs, to rebuke and threaten, and meditate and preach on hell fire and outer darkness rather than on the love and mercy of God, and on the glories of Paradise—a temper of mind which was perhaps a national characteristic, to culminate eventually in stern Calvinism.

This missionary, by name Corman, attempted in vain to preach the Gospel to the Northumbrians, who heard him with opposition and dislike. After some time he returned to Iona; and in rendering an account of his mission to the fathers of the monastery, he declared that he could make nothing of the Angles, that they were a race of untamable savages, and of a stubborn and barbarous spirit. This report greatly perplexed the fathers of the synod, who ardently desired to impart to the English people the gift of salvation which had been asked from them. They deliberated for a long time, until at length one of the assembly, Aidan, a monk of Iona, said to the discomfited preacher, "It seems to me, my brother, that you have been too hard on these ignorant people: you have not, according to the

[1] The greater part of this life is taken from Montalembert's Monks of the West.

apostolic counsel, offered them first the milk of gentle doctrine, to bring them by degrees, while nourishing them with the Divine Word, to the true understanding and practice of the more advanced precepts."

At these words every eye was turned to Aidan: his opinion was thoughtfully discussed, and the debate ended in an acknowledgment that he was the man wanted for the mission, since he was endowed with that discernment which is the source of all virtues. There was a bishop in the monastery of Iona, and Aidan received consecration from his hands for the work of God in Northumbria.

He received his mission from the whole brotherhood and from Seghen, Abbot of Iona, the fourth successor of Columba in the monastic metropolis of the Hebrides.

Aidan found that everything had to be done, or done over again, in the once Christian Northumbria. To the south, in Deira, the ravages of Cadwallon and Penda do not seem to have left any traces of the mission of Paulinus except the solitary church at York, where the deacon, James, had maintained the celebration of Christian worship, and which, begun by Edwin, was completed by Oswald. In Bernicia the Roman bishop, Paulinus, had restricted himself to itinerating missions, followed by general baptism, but he had not founded there any permanent station, since, until the Cross was planted by Oswald on the eve of his victory over the Britons, it is said that no one had ever seen a church, or an altar, or any emblem of the Christian faith.

It was thus a hard task, and one well wor thy of a followe of Columba, which presented itself to the monk of Iona, trained in the school of that great missionary.

Aidan had brought with him several of his brethren, and the number of Celtic monks who came to help him increased from day to day. It became necessary to assign to them, or rather to create for them, a centre of operations. The

King left to Aidan the choice of the seat of his bishopric. Although his diocese comprised the whole of Northumbria, he does not seem to have thought of occupying the vacant see of York. Whether he yielded in this to the prejudices and dislikes which separated the Scots from Roman usages, or whether he was unwilling to quit the northern district, where the mission of Paulinus had left the fewest traces, and where, consequently, he had most work to do, it is certain that he chose to place his episcopal monastery at a distance from the churches founded by the Roman monks in the southern part of the country.

He preferred a position a little more central, near the royal residence of Oswald, and on the coast, but much nearer the Firth of Forth than the mouth of the Humber, which mark the two extreme limits of Oswald's kingdom to the north and south.

This choice of a residence shows that, as a monk of Iona, ambitious of following in every respect the example of the great apostle of his race, founder of the sanctuary whence he issued, S. Aidan took pleasure in imitating S. Columba even in local particulars. Like him he settled his community in an island near the shore, almost as small, as insignificant, and as barren as Iona was when the holy exile from Ireland landed there. Its position was even, in some respects, a repetition, in the North Sea and to the East of Great Britain, of the position of Iona upon the opposite coast and on the shore of the Atlantic.

Amid the waves of the North Sea, opposite the green hills of Northumberland, and the sandy beach which extends between the border town of Berwick on the North, and the imposing scene of the feudal fortress of Bamborough on the South, lies a low island, flat and sombre, girt with basaltic rocks, forming a kind of square block, which terminates to the north-west in a long point of land stretching towards the mouth of the Tweed and Scotland. This island bears the impress of melancholy and barrenness. It can never have produced anything but the sorriest crops and some meagre pasturage. There is not a tree, not an undulation, not one noticeable feature, save a small conical hill to the south-west, now crowned by a strong castle of picturesque form but recent construction.

In this poor islet was erected the first Christian church of the whole district, now so populous, rich, and industrious, which extends from Hull to Edinburgh. This was Lindisfarne—that is to say, the Mother Church, the religious capital of the North of England and the South of Scotland, the residence of the first sixteen bishops of Northumbria, the sanctuary and monastic citadel of the whole country round—the Iona of the Anglo-Saxons. The resemblance of Lindisfarne to Iona, of the colony to the metropolis, the daughter to the mother, is striking. These two isles, once so celebrated, so renowned, so influential over two great hostile races, have the same sombre and melancholy aspect, full of a wild and savage sadness.

The island chosen by Aidan is, however, an island during only a portion of each day. As at S. Michael's Mount in Cornwall, twice in twenty-four hours the ebbing tide leaves the sands uncovered, and the passage can be made on foot to the neighbouring shore, though not always without danger, for many stories are told of travellers drowned in attempting to cross to the holy isle at low water.

From this new abode Aidan, looking southward, could descry far off the rock and stronghold of Bamborough, where Oswald, after the example of his grandfather Ida, had established his capital. His eye, like his heart, could there hail the young and glorious prince who was his friend, his helper, and his rival.

Nothing is told us by Bede of the early history of S. Aidan.

But the Irish Kalendars state that he was the son of Lugair, of the race of Eochaidh Finn Fuath-nairt, from whom S. Bridgit was descended. They state that he was bishop first at Inis Cathaigh (Scattery Isle, County Clare), but this is certainly a mistake. He may have resided there as a cenobite, but not as a bishop, before entering the community of Iona. When he first appears to us he is already a monk at Iona, and clothed with a certain authority among his brethren. Even when raised to the episcopate, he remained always a monk, not only in heart, but in life. Almost all his Celtic fellow-workers, whether from Ireland or Scotland, were monks like himself, and followed the cenobitical rule of their order and country. A hundred years after Aidan, the system which he had established at Lindisfarne was still in full vigour; and, as in his day, the bishop himself was either himself the abbot of the insular community, or lived there as a monk, subject, like the other religious, to the authority of the abbot, elected with the consent of the brotherhood. The priests, deacons, choristers, and other officials of the cathedral, were all monks. But this monastic discipline and order would have availed little if the missionary-head of the institution had not possessed the character common to great servants of the truth, and been endowed with those virtues which the apostolic office demands.

Bede, who was born twenty years after the death of the monk-bishop, and who lived all his life in the country which was fragrant with the memory of Aidan's virtues, has made his character and life the subject of one of the most eloquent and attractive pictures ever drawn by the pen of the venerable historian. The praise which he awards to him is not only more expressive and more distinct than that given to any other monastic apostle of England, but also so much the less to be suspected of partiality, that it is qualified by most energetic protests against the Celtic Church and its apostles for their fidelity to Celtic observances as to the celebration of Easter, which the clergy of the South of Ireland had abandoned out of deference to the Roman usage, but which the Scots of the North of Ireland and of all Caledonia obstinately preserved as they had received them from their fathers.

"Aidan was," Bede tells us, "a pontiff inspired with a passionate love of goodness; but at the same time full of a surpassing gentleness and moderation."

Faithful to all the noble teachings of his monastic cradle, he appeared to the future clergy of Northumbria as a marvel of self-denial and austerity. He was the first to practise what he taught, and none could ever reproach him with having failed to fulfil, to his best ability, all the precepts of the Gospels, of the apostles, and the prophets.

Indifferent to all worldly possessions, Aidan expended in alms all that he received from the kings and rich men. To the astonishment of the Saxons, who, like modern Englishmen, were excellent horsemen, and valued nothing more highly than the horse, it was always on foot that the bishop went through town and country, penetrating everywhere—now among the rich, now among the poor—baptizing those who were still heathen, confirming in the faith those who were already Christians, and stimulating all to alms-giving and good works. All who accompanied him, monks or laymen, had to devote a certain portion of each day to meditation—that is to say, to reading the Bible and learning the Psalter. Unwearied in study, humble and peaceful, charitable and sincere, he was especially distinguished by zeal against the sins of the rich. Far from sparing any of their vices or excesses, he rebuked them with the greatest sharpness; and contrary to the received custom, he never made any present to the chiefs or nobles, restricting himself to simple hospitality when they came to visit him, and giving away to the necessitous the gifts they heaped upon him. But the priestly courage which armed him against the pride of the powerful was transformed into a wonderful tenderness and watchful solicitude when he had to defend the feeble, to relieve the needy, or to comfort the unfortunate. His, in a word, was the heart of a true priest and apostle, disdainful alike of false grandeur and vain prosperity, and victorious over all the mean and perverse tendencies of his time, of all times.

Aidan retained nothing for himself of all the gifts of land which the generosity of the Saxon kings and nobles bestowed upon the Church, whose doctrines they had just embraced. He was content with Lindisfarne and the scanty fields of his poor little isle. But he reserved for himself, wherever it was possible, a site for a chapel, with a small chamber attached, where he prepared his sermons, and in which he lodged during his incessant and prolonged journeys.

Like S. Gregory the Great, whom, though not his disciple, he emulated in well-doing, he took an especial interest in the education of children and the emancipation of slaves. From the beginning of his mission he attached to himself twelve English youths, whom he educated with the greatest care for the service of Christ, and of whom at least one became a bishop. Every church and monastery founded by him became immediately a school where the children of the English received from Aidan's monks an education as complete as that to be had in any of the great Irish monasteries. As to slaves, he devoted principally to their redemption the gifts which he owed to the munificence of the Anglo-Saxons, endeavouring especially to save such as, to use Bede's expression, had been "unjustly sold"—which means, probably, those who were not foreign prisoners, or who had not been condemned to slavery as a punishment for crime.

For the Saxons, as well as the Celts, made no scruple of selling their brethren and children like cattle. The freedmen were carefully instructed by Aidan, numbered among his disciples, and frequently raised to the priesthood. Heathen barbarism was thus assailed and undermined in its very citadel by monks, both from the north and from the south, and by slaves promoted to the rank of priests.

An account of the united labours of S. Oswald and S. Aidan has been already given in this volume, and to it the reader is referred.[1]

The battle of Maserfield closed the life and good work of the blessed Oswald, one of the noblest, purest, and most earnest kings known to history.

Oswin claimed and seized on the throne of Deira, and Aidan was as much beloved and respected by this young prince as he had been by Oswald. The touching story of their intimacy and of the early death of Oswin has already found its place in this volume.[2] The fierce Penda, at the head of his Mercians and the Britons, for thirteen years ravaged Northumbria; but he seems to have entertained less unfriendly feelings towards his neighbours the Deirians and their king than to the Bernicians, and Oswy, the brother of Oswald, his last victim. It is in the north of the two kingdoms that we find him carrying everywhere fire and sword, and attempting to give to the flames the royal fortress of Bamborough. There also we find Aidan, the benefactor and protector of the country. Penda, not having been able to reduce the fortress either by assault or by investment, caused an enormous pile to be erected all round the rampart. He heaped on it all the wood of the surrounding forests, the drift wood from the beach, the beams, and even the thatch of the cottages in all the neighbouring villages which he had destroyed; then, as soon as the wind blew from the West, he set fire to

[1] Aug. 5, p. 70. [2] Aug. 20, p. 192.

the mass, with the hope of seeing the flames reach the town.

Aidan was at this time in the islet of Farne, an isolated rock in the open sea, a little to the south of Lindisfarne, and nearly opposite Bamborough, to which he often went, quitting his episcopal monastery to devote himself in solitude and silence to prayer. While he prayed he saw a cloud of black smoke and jets of flame covering the sky above the town where once his dear Oswald had dwelt. Lifting his eyes and hands to heaven, he cried with tears, "My God, behold all the evils that Penda does us!" At the same moment the wind changed, the flames whirled upon the besiegers, destroying many of them, and they speedily abandoned the siege of a place so evidently under Divine protection.

As if this formidable and pitiless enemy was not enough to desolate Northumbria, Oswy, moved by jealousy, made war against Oswin, King of the Deirians. Thus Northumberland was a prey to internecine war as well as desolation from the invasions of the ruthless Penda.

Oswin was defeated and put to death; and twelve days afterwards the glorious Bishop Aidan followed the king he loved to the tomb. He fell sick during one of his innumerable missionary expeditions, and died under a tent which had been pitched in haste to shelter him at the back of a modest church he had just built. He expired with his head resting against one of the buttresses of the church. It was a death which became a soldier of the faith upon his own fit field of battle.

The body of Aidan was laid in his monastic cathedral of Lindisfarne.

To Aidan far rather than to Augustine may England, certainly all the North, look as to her apostle.

S. FINAN, B. OF LINDISFARNE.

(A.D. 661.)

[Anglican Martyrology. Colgan in his Acts of the Irish Saints notes him on the same day. Same day in the Aberdeen Breviary, but Dempster says he was commemorated in Scotland on Feb. 16th. Among the Irish, Jan. 9th was regarded as a day on which S. Finan was honoured. Authority :—Bede, Hist. Eccl. lib. iii. c. 17, 21, 25, &c.]

ENGLAND was Christianized from two quarters ; Kent and all the south received the Gospel from Rome through the mission of S. Augustine ; but the whole of the north-east of the island, called Northumbria, including the modern Northumberland, Durham, and Yorkshire, was Christianized from Iona, the great monastery of S. Columba.

The first four successors of Augustine at Canterbury were all chosen from the Italian monks who had accompanied him to England ; but they all belonged to that first mission; whereas the See of Lindisfarne, as it became vacant, was filled from Iona. The Scottish monks, thus placed during thirty years at the head of the Church in the North of England, showed themselves worthy of the saintly school whence they issued, and of the glorious mission to which they were consecrated.

The first monk sent from Iona to replace the noble Aidan, (Oct. 22nd), was S. Finan. His episcopate was prosperous ; it lasted ten years, and was not interrupted by any melancholy event, such as those which had troubled the life of Aidan, by taking from him his two royal friends. S. Finan always lived on good terms with king Oswy, and before going to join his predecessor in heaven, he had the happiness of introducing to the Church the heads of the two great Saxon kingdoms. Sigebert, king of the East Saxons, and Peada, king of the Midland English, came to seek baptism at the gates of Lindisfarne. This made way to the conversion of their respective provinces, which this holy prelate furnished with proper missioners; and after some time, he ordained the Scot, Diuma, bishop of the Midland English, and S. Cedd (January 7th), bishop of the East Saxons. In the island sanctuary of Lindisfarne, S. Finan caused a cathedral to be built, not of stone, like that which Paulinus and Edwin had commenced at York, but according to the Keltic custom, and like the churches built by Columba and his Irish monks, it was made entirely of wood, and covered with bent, that long rough sea-grass, whose pivot-like roots bind together the sands on the sea-shore, and which is still found in great abundance on the island, as well as on the sandy beach which has to be crossed before the traveller can reach Lindisfarne.

Vast as was his diocese, which embraced the two great Northumbrian kingdoms, and great as must have been his influence over the other Saxon provinces, S. Finan seems to have preserved and exercised an authority not less complete over the country of his origin, the kingdom of the Dalriadian Scots. The Scotch annalists all speak of a certain king Fergus, who, by his violence and exactions, had raised the indignation of the Scottish clergy, and called down upon himself a sentence of excommunication from the bishops of Lindisfarne, Finan and his successors. Bede, who is prejudiced against this holy prelate, because of his adhesion to the Keltic ritual, and resistance of the introduction of the Roman usages in vogue in the South of England, nevertheless admits his great virtues, his contempt of the world, love of poverty and disinterestedness, and great diligence in preaching the Word of Life.[1]

[1] Montalembert: "Monks of the West."

S. CEADMON, MONK.

(ABOUT A.D. 680.)

[Anglican Martyrology, published by John Wilson. Authority:--Bede: Hist. Eccl. iv. 24.]

ACCORDING to an usage very general in the 7th century in England, but principally prevailing in Celtic countries, monasteries and nunneries were placed under the rule of one abbot or abbess. This was the case at Whitby, where the abbess Hilda governed a community of men, as well as one of women; and she inspired the monks subject to her authority with so great a devotion to their rule, so true a love of sacred literature, that this monastery, ruled by a woman, became a true school of missionaries, and even of bishops. But not all the bishops and saints nurtured in her school, occupy in the annals of the human mind a place comparable to that held by an old cowherd who lived on the lands belonging to Hilda's community. It is on the lips of this cowherd that Anglo-Saxon speech first bursts into poetry, and nothing in the whole history of European literature is more original or more religious than this first utterance of the English muse. His name was Ceadmon. He had already reached an advanced age, having spent his life in his humble occupation without ever learning music, or being able to join in the joyous choruses which held such a high place at the feasts and social gatherings of all classes, both poor and rich, among the Anglo-Saxons as among the Celts. When it was his turn to sing at any of these festal meetings, and the harp was handed to him, his custom was to rise from the table and go home. One evening, when he had thus withdrawn himself from his friends, he went back to his humble shed and went to sleep by the side of the cattle. During his slumber he heard a voice, which called him by name, and said to him, "Sing me something"; to which he replied, "I cannot sing, and that is why I have left the supper and am come hither." "Sing, notwithstanding," said the voice. "But what, then, shall I sing?" "Sing the beginning of the world: the Creation." Immediately on receiving this command he began to sing verses, of which before he had no knowledge, but which celebrated the glory and power of the Creator. On awaking he recollected all that he had sung in his dream, and hastened to tell all that had happened to him to the farmer in whose service he was.

The Abbess Hilda, when the story was repeated to her, called for Ceadmon and questioned him in the presence of all the learned men whom she could assemble around her. He was made to relate his vision and recite his songs, and then the different passages of sacred history and various points of doctrine were explained to him that he might put them into verse. The next morning he was again called, and immediately began to repeat all that had been told him, in verses, which were pronounced to be excellent. He was thus discovered all at once to possess the gift of improvisation in his mother tongue. Hilda, and her learned assessors, did not hesitate to recognise in this a special gift of God, worthy of all respect and of the most tender care. She received Ceadmon and his whole family within the monastic community of Whitby, and afterwards admitted him to the number of monks who were under her rule, and made him carefully translate the whole Bible into Anglo-Saxon. As soon, accordingly, as the sacred history and the gospel were narrated to him, he made himself master of the tale, ruminated it, as Bede said, and transformed it into songs, so beautiful that all who listened to him were delighted. He thus put into verse the whole of Genesis and Exodus, with other portions of the Old Testament, and, afterwards the life and passion of Our Lord, and the Acts of the Apostles. His talent and his poetic faculty thus went on, day by day, to fuller development, and he devoted numerous songs to such subjects as were best calculated to induce his companions to forsake evil, and love and practise the good: the terrors of the last judgment, the pains of hell, the joys of paradise—all these great and momentous subjects were in their turn woven into verse. The fragments that remain enable us to estimate the earnest and impassioned inspirations, strongly Christian and profoundly original, which characterised these first efforts of genius, barbarous, but subdued and baptized. But it would be a totally mistaken idea to recognise in the Abbess Hilda's dependant, nothing but a poet or a literary pioneer; he was, above all, a primitive Christian, a true monk, and, in one word, a saint. His mind was simple and humble, mild and pure; he served God with tranquil devotion, grateful for the extraordinary grace that he had received from heaven. But he was full of zeal for monastic regularity. No frivolous or worldly subjects ever inspired his verse; he composed his songs only that they might be useful to the soul, and their solemn beauty did even more for the conversion than for the delight of his countrymen. Many were moved by them to despise this world, and to turn with ardent love to the divine life. He died as poets seldom die. At the very beginning of his illness he desired his bed to be made in that part of the infirmary which was assigned to the dying, and, while smiling and talking cheerfully with his brethren, asked for the *viaticum*. At the moment when he was about to administer the Communion to himself, from the pyx brought from the Church, according to the usage of the period, and while holding in his hands the Holy Eucharist, he asked all those around him, if any one had any grudge against him, or any complaint to make? All answered, "No." Then said he, "I, too, my children, have a mind at peace with all God's servants." A little while after he had received the venerable Sacrament, as they were about to waken the monks for Matins, he made the sign of the Cross, laid his head on the pillow, and fell asleep in silence, to awake no more.

S. EBBA, V. ABSS.

(A.D. 683.)

[Wilson's Anglican Martyrology. Whitford and Greven, and other modern Martyrologists. Some confusion has arisen from there having been two S. Ebbas, both Abbesses of Coldingham, one commemorated at Coldingham on April 2, the other on Aug. 25. In Dempster's Scottish Menology on Aug. 22, but then he confounds the two Ebbas; he says S. Ebba, Virgin and Martyr, at Coldingham. Authorities:—Mention by Bede in his Ecc. Hist., and the Acts in Capgrave.]

At the northern extremity of Northumberland, beyond Lindisfarne, on what is now the frontier of Scotland, at Coldingham, rose two monasteries, one for men, the other for women—both founded and governed by one abbess. Whilst S. Hilda, the Deirian Princess, ruled her double monastery on the headland of Whitby, in her father's kingdom, Ebba, a princess of the rival dynasty, granddaughter of Ida the Burner, daughter of Ethelfrid the Ravager, but sister to S. Oswald and Oswy the reigning King of Bernicia, formed on the seacoast another monastic centre, which was yet to hold an important position, and to work out a stormy history.

It had been the intention of her brother to give her in marriage to the King of the Scots, but Ebba obstinately opposed the marriage. She received the veil from the hands of S. Finan, successor of the great Aidan at Lindisfarne; Oswy left her at liberty to devote herself to God, and gave her a piece of land on the banks of the Derwent, where she might found her first monastery, which received the name of Ebbchester—or Ebba's Castle. But the principal scene of her activities was Coldingham, in a situation which she seems to have chosen in emulation of that of Whitby. Hither, says tradition, she fled from the pursuit of her royal Scottish lover, and the sea at her bidding rolled along the valley between the headland and the mainland, and for three days checked the advance of the prince. She elicited also by her prayers two fountains of limpid water, one at the top of the hill, the other, which is perennial, at its base. S. Ebba's great and famous monastery was built on this promontory, now called after her S. Abb's Head, which abruptly terminates the range of the Lammermoors, thrusting itself out into the German ocean. From this headland, or rather precipice, which rises perpendicularly for more than 500 feet from the level of the sea, the view embraces on the north the Scottish coast to the farther side of the Forth, and, on the south, the English coast as far as the holy isle of Lindisfarne, and the royal acropolis of Bamborough. A small ruined chapel is all that remains to mark the site of the great sanctuary of Ebba, who was, like Hilda, placed at the head of a double community of men and women, and presided over the religious life of Northern Northumbria with no less success, and for an equal length of time, taking her part also, during nearly thirty years, with no less authority in the affairs of her country.

She did not always succeed, however, in maintaining amongst her daughters the fervour and gravity of which she herself gave an example. S. Etheldred of Ely was, for a while, her disciple; S. Cuthbert also learned there the danger of too close a proximity to women.[1] It was a blunder to combine under one roof monks and nuns. "The beauty of the virgins allured the men, and a restless desire to be after the men possessed the virgins,"[2] is the candid confession of the biographer of S. Ebba. No wonder then that after a brief sojourn at Coldingham, S. Cuthbert went off fully resolved "to avoid the society of women as a pest."

[1] "Beatus Cuthbertus intellecta confusione in domo Domini per feminas facta, creditur, etsi non legitur, celebre condidisse decretum lege perpetua servis suis observandum, quo non solum eis sui corporis præsentia, consortia fœminarum inhibuit, verum etiam introitus earum, et accessus et aspectus abscidit." *Vit. ap. Capgrave.*

[2] "Virginum species viros allexit, et inquieta virorum cupido virgines attraxit, et quasi stellæ de cœlo cadentes in ceno voluptatum involuti sunt." *Vit. ap. Capgrave.*

The saintly Abbess was warned of the relaxation which had crept into the monastery, by a holy priest of her community named Adamnan.[1] This man had been guilty of certain evil acts in his youth, and had gone to an old Irish priest for confession and advice. "What shall I do to make atonement for the past, and to save my soul in the Day of the Lord? Shall I spend my nights standing in prayer, and fast all the week save Sunday?" "It is too much," answered the Irish missionary; "fast twice or thrice a week. But I am going away to Ireland. On my return I will tell you my advice, I shall have time to think it over."

He went away and never returned, for he died in Ireland. Adamnan thenceforth lived in great strictness; he fasted every day save Sunday and Thursday, and spent the greater part of his nights in prayer. He afterwards became attached as priest to the establishment at Coldingham. As he went one day with the abbess through the vast and lofty buildings which she had erected on her headland, he said to her with tears, "All that you see here, so beautiful and so grand, will soon be laid in ashes." And as the astonished princess exclaimed against this prophecy, "Yes," he continued, "A strange man appeared to me in my visions at night, and revealed to me the evil that is done in this house, and the punishment that is prepared for it. He told me that he has visited each cell and each bed, and has found not one save thine as it should be. All, all the men and all the women are either fast asleep, or waking to mischief. Instead of praying and reading in their cells, they are organizing little picnics in them, with food and drink, or assembled for tittle-tattle.[2] The maidens, instead of meditating on divine

[1] Not Adamnan the historian and successor of S. Columba at Iona.

[2] "Omnes prorsus viri et feminæ aut somno torpent inerti, aut ad peccata vigilant: nam et domunculæ, quæ ad orandum vel legendum factæ erant, nunc in commessationum, potationum, fabulationum et ceterarum sunt illecebrarum cubilia conversæ." *Bede* iv. 25.

things, are weaving fine garments for their own persons or for their friends. Therefore a heavy vengeance from heaven is prepared against this house and against its inhabitants." "Why did you not tell me this before?" asked the surprised abbess. "I feared to do so," said Adamnan, "lest it should trouble you. But you have this consolation, that the destruction of the house will not take place in your days."

The vision having been divulged, the inmates of the double monastery were affected with compunction, and for a while[1] became demure and orderly in their conduct. But it did not last long. Shortly after S. Ebba died, and then all went on as before, and even worse, so that the burning of the monastery ended a scandal throughout the country. It does not speak much for the common sense of S. Ebba to have founded such an establishment, nor for her capability of governing, that she should have been profoundly ignorant of the disorders which took place under the same roof till enlightened by Adamnan. She was not a Hilda, able to rule and keep in propriety an institution with the elements of mischief existing in its very constitution. There is no report of frolicsomeness in the monks and nuns of Whitby. The scandals of Coldingham indicate the incapacity of the abbess, a worthy, devout woman, but occupying a position of extraordinary difficulty she had created for herself, and which she was utterly incompetent to fill—a feature not exceptional in weak people.

On April 2nd is commemorated another S. Ebba of Coldingham, abbess in A.D. 870, when the convent without the adjacent monastery had been re-erected, and a more orderly sisterhood filled it. In that year the Danes invaded Northumbria, and would have insulted the virgins of Coldingham and carried them to their homes as slaves and concubines, had not the maidens at the instigation of their

[1] "Aliquantulum."

S. BEGA, OR BEE, ABSS.

(END OF 7TH CENT.)

[Aberdeen Breviary, on October 31. The Anglican Martyrology of Wilson (A.D. 1608), and Dempster in his Scottish Menology. Authority:—A Life, late, from a MS. in the British Museum, pub. by Tomlinson, Carlisle, 1842. The following is from Montalembert's Monks of the West.]

IN Cumberland, upon a promontory bathed by the waves of the Irish sea, and from which in clear weather the southern shore of Scotland and the distant peaks of the Isle of Man may be seen, a religious edifice still bears the name and preserves the recollection of S. Bega. She was, according to the legend, the daughter of an Irish king, the most beautiful woman in the country, and already asked in marriage by the son of the King of Norway. But she had vowed herself, from her tenderest infancy, to the spouse of virgins, and had received from an angel, as a seal of her celestial betrothal, a bracelet marked with the sign of the cross. On the night before her wedding-day, while the guards of the king her father, instead of keeping watch, as usual, with sabres at their sides and axes on their shoulders, were, like their guests, deep in the revel, she escaped alone, with nothing but the bracelet which the angel had given her, threw herself upon a green sod, and was wafted to the opposite shore, in Northumberland, where she lived long in a cell in the wood, uniting with her prayers the care of the sick poor around. Fear of the pirates who infested these coasts led her, after awhile, farther inland. What then became of her? Here the confusion, which is so general in the debateable ground between legend and history, becomes nearly inextricable. Was it she who, under the name of Heïu, is pointed out to us by Beda as the woman to whom Bishop Aïdan, the apostle of Northumbria, gave the veil, and whom he placed at the head of the first nunnery which had been seen in the north of England? Or was it she who, under the name of Bega, after having abdicated the dignity of abbess, lived for thirty years a humble and simple nun in one of the monasteries under the rule of the great Abbess of Whitby, Hilda, whose intimate friend she became, as well as her daughter in religion?

These are questions which have been long disputed by the learned, and which it seems impossible to bring to any satisfactory conclusion. What is certain, however, is that a virgin of the name of Bega figures among the most well-known and long venerated saints of the north-west of England. She was celebrated during her lifetime for her austerity, her fervour, and an anxiety for the poor, which led her, during the building of her monastery, to prepare with her own hands the food of the masons, and to wait upon them in their workshops, hastening from place to place like a bee laden with honey. She remained down to the Middle Ages the patroness of the laborious and often oppressed population of the district, in which tradition presents her to us as arriving alone and fearless on a foreign shore, flying from her royal bridegroom. In the twelfth century the famous bracelet which the angel had given her was regarded with tender veneration; the pious confidence of the faithful turned it into a relic upon which usurpers, prevaricators, and oppressors against whom there existed no other defence, were made to swear, with the certainty that a perjury committed on so dear and sacred a pledge would not pass unpunished. It was also to Bega and her bracelet that the cultivators of the soil had recourse against the new and unjust taxes with which their lords burdened them. In vain the Scottish rievers or the *prepotents* of the country, treading down under their horses' feet the harvest of the Cumbrians, made light of the complaints and threats of the votaries of S. Bega. "What is the good old woman to me, and what harm can she do me?" said one. "Let your Bega come!" said another—"let her come and do whatever she likes!

she cannot make one of our horses cast his shoes." Sooner or later divine vengeance struck these culprits; and the fame of the chastisements sent upon them confirmed the faith of the people in the powerful intercession of her who, six hundred years after her death, still gave a protection effectual and energetic against feudal rudeness, to the captive and to the oppressed, to the chastity of women, and the rights of the lowly, upon the western shore of Northumbria.

S. EATA, AB., B. OF HEXHAM.

(A.D. 685.)

[Dempster, in his Scottish Menology, on May 7. Menardus, in his Benedictine Martyrology, on Oct. 26; Bollandists on same day. Authorities :—Mention by Bede; and a Life, written in the 12th cent., by an anonymous author.]

WHEN S. Aidan was summoned from his monastic seclusion at Iona to do the work of an apostle in Northumbria, from the beginning of his mission he attached to himself twelve English youths, whom he educated with the greatest care for the service of Christ, and of whom one, Eata, became a bishop. Eata, as Bede tells us, "a meek and simple man," was first Abbot of Melrose, where he guided the youth of the great Cuthbert. In 678, when Wilfred was driven from his see, two dioceses were constituted out of his see, one of the Bernicians, the seat of which was Hexham or Lindisfarne; the other over the Deiri with the seat at York. Eata was consecrated Bishop of Hexham, and Bosa was consecrated to York. At the same time Lindsey was made

[1] Myvyrian Archæology, i. pp. 1-14; 581-584. [2] *Ibid.* pp. 14-17.

the seat of a bishopric, and Edhed appointed to it. All three were consecrated by Archbishop Theodore at York. Eata brought Cuthbert with him from Melrose, and constituted him provost of the island monastery of Lindisfarne. Apparently Theodore designed a still further division of the diocese, Lindisfarne and Hexham to be erected into separate dioceses, for three years after Tumbert was appointed Bishop of Hexham, and Eata retained the bishopric and abbacy of Lindisfarne. But three years after, for some fault of disobedience, Tumbert was deposed and Cuthbert placed in his room. After a while, however, Cuthbert and Eata changed places, and shortly after his return to Hexham, Eata died.

In 1113 Thomas, Archbishop of York, went to Hexham with the design of removing the body of the old prelate to his own church. But in the night S. Eata appeared to him, staff in hand, and sternly said, "Why will you not let me rest in the church I governed, but will remove me to another church?" Then raising his staff, he smote him on the shoulder, and the archbishop awoke suffering from rheumatism, and resolved to let Eata alone.

PECTORAL CROSS OF ST. CUTHBERT.

S. HILDA, V. ABSS.

(ABOUT A.D. 679.)

[Gallican Martyrologies on this day. York Kalendar on Aug. 25. The Horæ B.V.M., probably belonging to Coldingham (Harl. MSS. 1804), and the Durham Missal "ad altare S. Joh. B. et S. Margaretæ, ad ix altaria in eccl. cath. Dunelm" (Harleian MSS. 5289), on Nov. 17. Authority :—Bede, Hist. Eccl.]

THE monastery of Hartlepool was founded about the year 645 by Heiu, a Northumbrian lady, the first woman of her race who embraced conventual life. She received the veil from the hands of Bishop Aidan. After a few years she retired to a solitude, and Aidan replaced her by Hilda, a princess of the blood-royal and of the Deirian dynasty. She was grand niece of Edwin, the first Christian king of Northumbria, father of the queen who had shared the throne of Oswy. This illustrious lady seemed to be called by her genius and character, even more than by her rank, to exercise a great influence over religious and political movements in her time. Born in exile, during the sovereignty of Ethelfrid, among the West Saxons, where her mother died a violent death, she returned with her father, on the restoration of his race in 617. In her early youth she had been baptized, with her uncle King Edwin, by the Roman missionary Paulinus, which did not, however, prevent her from leaning during her whole life to the side of the Celtic missionaries. Before consecrating her virginity to God, she had lived thirty-three years " very nobly," says Bede, among her family and her fellows. When she understood that God called her, she desired to make to Him a complete sacrifice, and forsook at once the world, her family, and her country. She went immediately into East Anglia, the king of which had married her sister, and whence she designed to cross over to France, in order to take the veil either at Chelles, where her widowed sister was one day to devote herself to God, or in one of the monasteries on the banks of the Marne, which sprang from the great Irish colony of Luxeuil, and whither the Saxon virgins already began to resort. Gallican martyrologists commemorate Hilda as having been some time at Chelles; but Bede says nothing of the sort. He implies that she did not go thither, but only wished to do so, and before she left East Anglia for Chelles received her recall to Northumbria from Bishop Aidan. She was only a year in all away from her native province. Aidan gave her lands by the Wear, and there she spent a twelvemonth with a few companions, till Heiu retired from governing Hartlepool, when Aidan made Hilda superior of the monastery. Probably Heiu had not ruled very well, for we are told that one of the first things done by Hilda was to introduce order into the monastery.

Nine years later, when the peace and freedom of Northumbria had been secured by the final victory gained by King Oswy over the Mercians, Hilda took advantage of a gift of land granted her by that prince to establish a new monastery at Streaneshalch (the Beacon Headland), now Whitby. There, as at Hartlepool, and during the thirty years that she passed at the head of her two houses, she displayed a rare capacity for the government of souls, and for the consolidation of monastic institutions. This special aptitude, joined to her love of monastic regularity, and her zeal for knowledge and ecclesiastical discipline, gave her an important part to play, and great influence. Her society was sought by S. Aidan, and all the religious who knew her, that they might be guided by her clear judgment and wise experience. Kings even, and princes of her blood, or of the adjacent provinces, often came to consult her, asking enlightenment, which they afterwards joyfully acknowledged themselves to have received. But she did not reserve the treasures of her judgment and charity for the great ones of the earth. She scattered round her everywhere the benefits of justice, piety, peace, and temperance. She was ere long regarded and honoured as the mother of her country, and all who addressed her gave her the sweet name of Mother, which she well deserved. Not only in Northumbria, but in distant regions, to which the fame of her virtue and enlightenment had penetrated, she was to many the instrument of their salvation and conversion. And in her two communities especially she secured, during a rule of more than thirty years, the supremacy of order, union, charity, and equality, so much, that it became usual to say to the proud Northumbrians, that the image of the primitive Church, wherein was neither rich nor poor, and where all was common among the Christians, was realized at Whitby.

But the most touching particular of all in the enthusiastic narrative of the Venerable Bede, is that which proves the passionate tenderness felt for her by her daughters, especially by the young girls whom she prepared for religious life in a separate house, by the discipline of a novitiate establishment regularly constituted and attentively superintended.

Nor did the royal abbess confine herself to the government of a numerous community of nuns. According to a usage then very general, but principally prevailing in the Celtic countries, a monastery was joined to the nunnery. And Hilda inspired the monks subject to her authority with so great a devotion to the rule, so true a love of sacred literature, so careful a study of the Scriptures, that this monastery, ruled by a woman, became a school of missionaries and bishops. Bosa of York, Hedda of Dorchester, Oftgar of Worcester, S. John of Beverley, Bishop of York, and Wilfrid, the disturber of her declining days, issued from her nursery of great men.

S. HILDA.

The poor cowherd Caedmon was reared into an ecclesiastical poet under her care, and became the father of English poetry.

In 664, Oswy convoked the council of Whitby to regulate and terminate the dispute raised by Wilfrid. This saint was fired with ambition to bring the Northumbrian Church into conformity with Roman practices. When appointed abbot of Ripon by Alcfrid, he turned out the monks because they would not give up their customs for those which he wished to introduce. Chief among the differences was the time for the observance of Easter. The Celtic Church had their calendar out of gear, and observed the queen of feasts before the time when it was celebrated by the Roman Church.

Hilda was fifty years old when the gathering at Whitby took place. She and her whole community clung to the Celtic tradition, and the national party was headed by Colman, bishop of Lindisfarne, supported by S. Cedd, then only a monk. Alcfrid and the queen favoured Wilfrid and Roman observance. An account of the assembly has been given elsewhere. King Oswy decided in favour of Wilfrid; Colman protested, refused to recognize the decision, and returned to Lindisfarne, collected the bones of S. Aidan, and departed for Iona. Wilfrid triumphed. He was appointed bishop of Northumbria, and then, to show his scorn for the Anglo-Saxon bishops, went to France to receive ordination from the Bishop of Paris. On his way back he was shipwrecked. When he returned, he found that his conduct had roused disgust and opposition. King Oswy had appointed in his room the holy bishop Chad. The Northumbrians, though they observed the decree of Whitby as to the celebration of Easter, refused to have such a firebrand as Wilfrid among them as bishop. There can be little doubt that this, to a great extent, was due to the advice of S. Hilda, who, as long as she lived, never relaxed her opposition to Wilfrid. Chad was afterwards removed to Mercia, and Wilfrid reinstated. But his violence and pride made his presence intolerable, and S. Theodore, archbishop of Canterbury, divided his diocese into three, A.D. 678, and gave York to Bosa, one of the disciples of S. Hilda, who in her monastery at Whitby, was now at a great age, but had not lost her influence, or her antipathy to Wilfrid. Wilfrid, incensed to the last degree, went to Rome to appeal to Pope Agatho against this subdivision of his huge diocese into workable parcels. It was done for the good of the Church, but it offended Wilfrid's pride. S. Hilda, the abbess, and S. Theodore, the archbishop, sent messengers to Rome to complain of Wilfrid's insolence. The council of Rome confirmed the division of the diocese, but ordered the reappointment of Wilfrid to one of the sees, that of York. King Egfrid called a council, the pontifical bulls were read, but instead of submitting, with the consent of Archbishop Theodore, the king imprisoned Wilfrid, and refused to carry out the orders of the Pope.

Hilda was dead before the strife ended. During the last six years of her life she suffered much from fever. But "during all this while she never failed either to return thanks to her Maker, or publicly and privately to instruct the flock committed to her charge." When dying, she called her monks and nuns around her, at early cock-crow, and, after exhorting them to preserve evangelical peace among themselves and towards all men, she passed by death to life eternal.

S. CUTHBERT reasoning with the monks.

S. CUTHBERT, B. OF LINDISFARNE.

(A.D. 687.)

[Martyrologies of Bede, Usuardus, Ado, Rabanus Maurus; the Anglican, Scottish, and Irish Martyrologies; the Benedictine and the Roman as well. Authorities:—Bede's Life of S. Cuthbert, another by a monk of Lindisfarne, written in the reign of Egfrid (d. 705). The following life is extracted from Montalembert's "Monks of the West."]

Of the parentage of Cuthbert, nothing for certain is known. The Kelts have claimed him as belonging to them, at least by birth. They made him out to have been the son of an Irish princess, reduced to slavery, like Bridget, the holy patroness of Ireland, but who fell, more miserably, victim to the lust of her savage master. His Celtic origin would seem to be more conclusively proved by his attitude towards S. Wilfrid, the introducer of Roman uniformity into the north of England, than by the tradition of the Anglo-Saxon monks of Durham. His name is certainly Saxon, and not Keltic. But, to tell the truth, nothing is certainly known either of his place of birth, or the rank of his family.

His first appearance in history is as a shepherd in Lauderdale, a valley watered by a river which flows into the Tweed near Melrose. It was then a district annexed to the kingdom of Northumbria, which had just been delivered by the holy king Oswald from the yoke of the Mercians and Britons. As he is soon afterwards to be seen travelling on horseback, lance in hand, and accompanied by a squire, it is not to be supposed that he was of poor extraction. At the same time, it was not the flocks of his father which he kept, as did David in the plains of Bethlehem; it is expressly noted that the flocks confided to his care belonged to a master, or to several masters. His family must have been in the rank of those vassals to whom the great Saxon lords gave the care and superintendence of their flocks upon the vast extent of pastures which, under the name of *folc-land* or common, was left to their use, and where the cow-herds and shepherds lived day and night in the open air, as is still done by the shepherds of Hungary.

Popular imagination in the north of England, of which Cuthbert was the hero before, as well as after, the Norman Conquest, had thus full scope in respect to the obscure childhood of its favourite saint, and delighted in weaving stories of his childish sports, representing him as walking on his hands, and turning somersaults with his little companions. A more authentic testimony, that of his contemporary, Bede, informs us that our shepherd boy had not his equal among the children of his age, for activity, dexterity, and boldness in the race and fight. In all sports and athletic exercises he was the first to challenge his companions, with the certainty of being the victor. The description reads like that of a little Anglo-Saxon of our own day—a scholar of Eton or Harrow. At the same time, a precocious piety showed itself in him, even amid the exuberance of youth. One night, as he said his prayers, while keeping the sheep of his master, he saw the sky, which had been very dark, broken by a track of light, upon which a cloud of angels descended from heaven, returning afterwards with a resplendent soul, which they had gone to meet on earth. Next morning he heard that Aidan, the holy bishop of Lindisfarne, the apostle of the district, had died during the night. This vision determined his monastic vocation.

Some time afterwards we find him at the gates of the monastery of Melrose, the great Keltic establishment for novices in Northumbria. He was then only fifteen, yet, nevertheless, he arrived on horseback, lance in hand, attended by a squire, for he had already begun his career in the battle-field, and learned in the face of the enemy the first lessons of abstinence, which he now meant to practise in the cloister. He was received by two great doctors of the Keltic Church,—the abbot Eata, one of the twelve Northumbrians first chosen by Aidan, and the prior Boswell, who conceived a special affection for the new-comer, and undertook the charge of his monastic education. Five centuries later, the copy of the Gospels in which the master and pupil had read daily, was still kissed with veneration in the cathedral of Durham.

The robust and energetic youth very soon showed the rarest aptitude for monastic life, not only for cenobitical exercises, but, above all, for the missionary work, which was the principal occupation of monks in that country and period. He was not content merely to surpass all the other monks in his devotion to the four principal occupations of monastic life—study, prayer, vigil, and manual labour—but speedily applied himself to the work of casting out from the hearts of the surrounding population the last vestiges of pagan superstition. Not a village was so distant, not a mountain side so steep, not a village so poor, that it escaped his zeal. He sometimes passed weeks, and even months, out of his monastery, preaching to and confessing the rustic population of the mountains. The roads were very bad, or rather there were no roads; only now and then was it possible to travel on horseback; sometimes, when his course lay along the coast of the district inhabited by the Picts, he would take the help of a boat. But generally it was on foot that he had to penetrate into the glens and distant valleys, crossing the heaths and vast table-lands, uncultivated and uninhabited, where a few shepherd's huts, like that in which he himself had passed his childhood, and which were in winter abandoned even by the rude inhabitants, were thinly scattered. But neither the intemperance of the seasons, nor hunger, nor thirst, arrested the young and valiant missionary in his apostolic travels, to seek the scattered population, half Celts, and half Anglo-Saxons, who, though already Christian in name and by baptism, retained an obstinate attachment to many of their ancient superstitions, and who were quickly led back by any great calamity, such as one of the great pestilences which were then so frequent, to the use of magic, amulets, and other practices of idolatry. The details which have been preserved of the wonders which often accompanied his wanderings, show that his labours extended over all the hilly district between the two seas—from the Solway to the Forth. They explain to us how the monks administered the consolations and the teaching of religion, before the organization of parishes, ordained by archbishop Theodore, had been everywhere introduced or regulated. As soon as the arrival of one of these apostolic missionaries in a somewhat central locality was known, all the population of the neighbourhood hastened to hear him, endeavouring with fervour and simplicity to put in practice the instruction they received from him. Cuthbert, especially, was received among them with affectionate confidence; his eloquence was so persuasive that it brought the most rebellious to his feet, to hear their sins revealed to them, and to accept the penance which he imposed upon them.

Cuthbert prepared himself for preaching and the administration of the Sacraments, by extraordinary penances and austerities. Stone bathing-places, in which he passed the entire night in prayer, lying in the frozen water, according to a custom common among the Keltic saints, are still shown in several different places. When he was near the sea, he went to the shore, unknown to any one, at night, and plunging into the waves up to his neck, sang his vigils there. As soon as he came out of the water he resumed his prayers on the sand of the beach. On one occasion, one of his disciples, who had followed him secretly in order to discover the aim of this nocturnal expedition, saw two otters come up out of the water, which, while the saint prayed on his knees, lick his frozen feet, and wipe them with their hair, until life and warmth returned to the benumbed members. By one of those strange caprices of human frivolity which disconcert the historian, this insignificant incident is the only recollection which now remains in the memory of the people. S. Cuthbert is known to the peasant of Northumberland and of the Scottish borders only by the legend of those compassionate otters.

He had been some years at Melrose, when the abbot Eata took him along with him to join the community of Keltic monks established by king Alchfrid at Ripon. Cuthbert held the office of steward, and in this office showed the same zeal as in his missions. When travellers arrived through the snow, famished and nearly fainting with cold, he himself washed their feet and warmed them against his bosom, then hastened to the oven to order bread to be made ready, if there was not enough.

Cuthbert returned with his countrymen to Melrose, resumed his life of missionary preaching, and again met his friend and master, the prior Boswell, at whose death, in the great pestilence of 664, Cuthbert was elected abbot in his place. He had been himself attacked by the disease; and all the monks prayed earnestly that his life might be preserved to them. When he knew that the community had spent the night in prayer for him, though he felt no better, he cried to himself, with a double impulse of his habitual energy, "What am I doing in bed? It is impossible that God should shut His ears to such men. Give me my staff and my shoes." And getting up, he immediately began to walk, leaning upon his staff. But this sudden cure left him subject to weakness, which shortened his life.

However, he had not long to remain at Melrose. The triumph of Wilfrid and the Roman ritual at the conference of Whitby, brought about a revolution in the monastic metropolis of Northumbria, and in the mother monastery of Melrose, at Lindisfarne. Bishop Colman had returned to Iona, carrying with him the bones of S. Aidan, the first apostle of the country, and followed by all the monks who would not consent to sacrifice their Keltic tradition to Roman unity. It was of importance to preserve the holy island, the special sanctuary of the country, for the religious family of which its foundress had been a member. Abbot Eata of Melrose undertook this difficult mission. He became abbot of Lindisfarne, and was invested with a kind of episcopal supremacy. He took with him the young Cuthbert, who was not yet thirty, but whom, however, he held alone capable of filling the important office of prior in the great insular community.

The struggle into which Eata and Cuthbert, in their own persons, had entered against Wilfrid, on the subject of Roman rites, did not point them out as the best men to introduce the novelties so passionately defended and insisted upon by the new bishop of Northumbria. Notwithstanding, everything goes to prove that the new abbot and prior of Lindisfarne adopted without reserve the decisions of the assembly of Whitby, and took serious pains to introduce them into the great Keltic community. Cuthbert, in whom the physical energy of a robust organization was united to an unconquerable gentleness, employed in this task all the resources of his mind and heart. All the rebels had not left with bishop Colman; some monks still remained, who held obstinately by their ancient customs. Cuthbert reasoned with them daily in the meetings of the chapter; his desire was to overcome their objections by patience and moderation alone; he bore their reproaches as long as that was possible, and when his endurance was at an end, raised the sitting without changing countenance or tone, and resumed next morning the course of the debate, without ever permitting himself to be moved to anger, or allowing any thing to disturb the inestimable gift of kindness and light heartedness which he had received from God.

But his great desire was the strict observance of the rule when once established; and his historian boasts, as one of his most remarkable victories, the obligation he imposed for ever upon the monks of Lindisfarne of wearing a simple and uniform dress, in undyed wool, and thus giving up the passionate liking of the Anglo-Saxons for varied and brilliant colours.

During the twelve years which he passed at Lindisfarne, the life of Cuthbert was identical with that which he had led at Melrose. Within doors this life was spent in the severe practice of all the austerities of the cloister, in manual labour, united to the punctual celebration of divine worship, and such fervour in prayer that he often slept only one night in the three or four, passing the others in prayer, and in singing the service alone while walking round the aisle to keep himself awake. Outside, the same zeal for preaching, the same solicitude for the salvation and well-being, temporal as well as spiritual, of the Northumbrian people, was apparent in him. He carried to them the Word of Life; he soothed their sufferings, by curing miraculously a crowd of diseases which were beyond the power of the physicians. But the valiant missionary specially assailed the diseases of the soul, and made use of all the tenderness and all the ardour of his own spirit to reach them. When he celebrated mass before the assembled crowd, his visible emotion, his inspired looks, his trembling voice, all contributed to penetrate and over-power the multitude. The Anglo-Saxon Christians, who came in crowds to open their hearts to him in the confessional, were still more profoundly impressed.

Though he was a bold and inflexible judge of impenitent vice, he felt and expressed the tenderest compassion for the contrite sinner. He was the first to weep over the sins which he pardoned in the name of God; and he himself fulfilled the penances which he imposed as the conditions of absolution, thus gaining by his humility the hearts which he longed to convert and cure.

But neither the life of a cenobite, nor the labours of a missionary could satisfy the aspirations of his soul after perfection. When he was not quite forty, after holding his priorship at Lindisfarne for twelve years, he resolved to leave monastic life, and to live as a hermit in a sterile and desert island, visible from Lindisfarne, which lay in the centre of the Archipelago, south of the holy isle, and almost opposite the fortified capital of the Northumbrian kings at Bamborough. No one dared to live on this island, which was called Farne, in consequence of its being supposed to be the haunt of demons. Cuthbert took possession of it as a soldier of Christ, victorious over the tyranny of evil, and built there a palace worthy of himself, hollowing out of the living rock a cell from which he could see nothing but the sky, that he might not be disturbed in his contemplations. The hide of an ox suspended before the entrance of his cavern, and which he turned according to the direction of the wind, afforded him a poor defence against the intemperance of that wild climate. His holy historian tells us that he exercised sway over the elements and brute creation as a true monarch of the land which he had conquered for Christ, and with that sovereign empire over nature which sin alone has taken from us. He lived on the produce of a little field of barley sown and cultivated by his own hands, but so small that the inhabitants of the coast reported among themselves that he was fed by angels with bread made in Paradise.

S. CUTHBERT
In His Hermit's Cell.

DEATH OF S. CUTHBERT. March 20.

The legends of Northumbria linger lovingly upon the solitary sojourn of their great national and popular saint in this basaltic isle. They attribute to him the extraordinary gentleness and familiarity of a particular species of aquatic birds which came when called, allowed themselves to be taken, stroked, caressed, and whose down was of remarkable softness. In ancient times they swarmed about this rock, and they are still to be found there, though much diminished in number since curious visitors have come to steal their nests and shoot the birds. These sea fowl are found nowhere else in the British Isles, and are called the *Birds of S. Cuthbert.* It was he, according to the narrative of a monk of the thirteenth century, who inspired them with a hereditary trust in man by taking them as companions of his solitude, and guaranteeing to them that they should never be disturbed in their homes.

It is he, too, according to the fishers of the surrounding islands, who makes certain little shells of the genus *Entrochus*, which are only to be found on this coast, and which have received the name of S. Cuthbert's Beads. They believe that he is still to be seen by night seated on a rock, and using another as an anvil for his work.

The pious anchorite, however, in condemning himself to the trials of solitude, had no intention of withdrawing from the cares of fraternal charity. He continued to receive frequent visits, in the first place from his neighbours and brethren at Lindisfarne, and in addition from all who came to consult him upon the state of their souls, as well as to seek consolation from him in adversity. The number of these pilgrims of sorrow was countless. They came not only from the neighbouring shores, but from the most distant provinces. Throughout all England the rumour spread, that on a desert rock of the Northumbrian coast there lived a solitary who was the friend of God, and skilled in the healing of human suffering. In this expectation no one was deceived; no man carried back from the sea-beaten island the same burden of suffering, temptation, or remorse which he had taken there. Cuthbert had consolation for all troubles, light for all the sorrowful mysteries of life, counsel for all its perils, a helping hand to all the hopeless, a heart open to all who suffered. He could draw from all terrestrial anguish a proof of the joys of heaven, deduce the certainty of those joys from the terrible evanescence of both good and evil in this world, and light up again in sick souls the fire of charity—the only defence, he said, against those ambushes of the old enemy which always take our hearts captive when they are emptied of divine and brotherly love.

To make his solitude more accessible to these visitors, and above all to his brethren from Lindisfarne, he had built some distance from the cave which was his dwelling, at a place where boats could land their passengers, a kind of *parlour* and refectory for the use of his guests. There he himself met, conversed, and ate with them, especially when, as he has himself told, the monks came to celebrate with him such a great feast as Christmas. At such moments he went freely into all their conversations and discussions, interrupting himself from time to time to remind them of the necessity of watchfulness and prayer. The monks answered him, "Nothing is more true; but we have so many days of vigil, of fasts and prayers. Let us at least to-day rejoice in the Lord." The Venerable Bede, who has preserved to us the precious memory of this exchange of brotherly familiarity has not disdained to tell us also of the reproaches addressed by Cuthbert to his brothers for not eating a fat goose which he had hung on the partition-wall of his guest's refectory, in order that they might thoroughly fortify themselves before they embarked upon the stormy sea to return to their monastery.

This tender charity and courteous activity were united in him to treasures of humility. He would not allow any one to suspect him of ranking the life of an anchorite above that of a member of a community. "It must not be supposed," he said, "because I prefer to live out of reach of every secular care, that my life is superior to that of others. The life of good cenobites, who obey their abbot in everything, and whose time is divided between prayer, work, and fasting is much to be admired. I know many among them whose souls are more pure, and their graces more exalted than mine; especially, and in the first rank my dear old Boswell, who received and trained me at Melrose in my youth."

Thus passed, in that dear solitude, and among these friendly surroundings, eight pleasant years, the sweetest of his life, and precisely those during which all Northumberland was convulsed by the struggle between Wilfrid and the new king Egfrid.

Then came the day upon which the king of the Northumbrians, accompanied by his principal nobles, and almost all the community of Lindisfarne, landed upon the rock of Farne, to beg, kneeling, and with tears, that Cuthbert would accept the episcopal dignity to which he had just been promoted in the synod of Twyford, presided over by archbishop Theodore. He yielded only after a long resistance, himself weeping when he did so. It was, however, permitted to him to delay his consecration for six months, till Easter, which left him still a winter in his dear solitude, before he went to York, where he was consecrated by the primate Theodore, assisted by six bishops. He would not, however, accept the diocese of Hexham, to which he had been first appointed, but persuaded his friend Eata, the bishop and abbot of Lindisfarne, to give up to him the monastic bishopric, where he had already lived so long.

The diocese of Lindisfarne spread far to the west, much beyond Hexham. The Britons of Cumbria who had come to be tributaries of the Northumbrian kings, were thus included in it. King Egfrid's deed of gift, in which he gives the district of Cartmell, with all the Britons who dwell in it, to bishop Cuthbert, still exists. The Roman city of Carlisle, transformed into an Anglo-Saxon fortress, was also under his sway, with all the surrounding monasteries.

His new dignity made no difference in his character, nor even in his mode of life. He retained his old habits as a cenobite, and even as a hermit. In the midst of his episcopal pomp he remained always the monk and missionary of old. His whole episcopate, indeed, seems to bear the character of a mission indefinitely prolonged. He went over his vast diocese, to administer confirmation to converts, traversing a crowd more attentive and respectful than ever, lavishing upon it all kinds of benefits, alms, clothing, sermons, miraculous cures—penetrating as of old into hamlets and distant corners, climbing the hills and downs, sleeping under a tent, and sometimes indeed finding no other shelter than in the huts of branches, brought from the nearest wood to the desert, in which he had made the torrent of his eloquence and charity to gush forth.

Here also we find illustrations, as at all previous periods of his life, of the most delightful feature of his good and holy soul. In the obscure missionary of Melrose, in the already celebrated prior of Lindisfarne, and still more, if that is possible, in the powerful and venerated bishop, the same heart, overflowing with tenderness and compassion is always to be found. The supernatural power given to him to cure the most cruel diseases was wonderful. But in his frequent and friendly intercourse with the great Anglo-

Saxon earls, the *ealdormen*, as well as with the mixed populations of Britons, Picts, Scots, and English, whom he gathered under his crosier, the principal feature in the numerous and detailed narratives which remain to us, and which gives to them a beauty as of youth, always attractive, is his intense and active sympathy for those human sorrows which in all ages are the same, always so keen, and capable of so little consolation. The more familiar the details of these meetings between the heart of a saint and true priest, and the simple and impetuous hearts of the first English Christians, the more attractive do they become, and we cannot resist the inclination of presenting to our readers some incidents which shew at once the liveliness of domestic affections among those newly-baptized barbarians and their filial and familiar confidence in their master. One of the ealdormen of king Egfrid arrived one day in breathless haste at Lindisfarne, overwhelmed with grief, his wife, a woman as pious and generous as himself, having been seized with a fit of violent madness. But he was ashamed to disclose the nature of the attack, it seemed to him a sort of chastisement from heaven, disgracing a creature hitherto so chaste and honoured; all that he said was that she was approaching death; and he begged that a priest might be given him to carry to her the viaticum, and that when she died he might be permitted to bury her in the holy isle. Cuthbert heard his story, and said to him with much emotion, "This is my business; no one but myself can go with you." As they rode on their way together, the husband wept, and Cuthbert, looking at him and seeing the cheeks of the rough warrior wet with tears, divined the whole; and during all the rest of the journey consoled and encouraged him, explaining to him that madness was not a punishment of crime, but a trial which God inflicted sometimes upon the innocent. "Besides," he added, "when we arrive we shall find her cured; she will come to meet us, and will help me to dismount from my horse, taking, according to her custom, the reins in her hand." And so the event proved; for, says that historian, the demon did not dare to await the coming of the Holy Ghost, of which the man of God was full. The noble lady, delivered from her bondage, rose as if from a profound sleep, and stood on the threshold to greet the holy friend of the house, seizing the reins of his horse, and joyfully announcing her sudden cure.

On another occasion, a certain count Henma, from whom he sought hospitality during one of his pastoral journeys, received him on his knees, thanking him for his visit, but at the same time telling him that his wife was at the point of death, and he himself in despair. "However," said the count, "I firmly believe that were you to give her your blessing, she would be restored to health, or at least delivered by a speedy death from her long and cruel sufferings." The saint immediately sent one of his priests, without entering into the sick room himself, to sprinkle her with water which he had blessed. The patient was at once relieved; and herself came to act as cupbearer to the prelate, offering him, in the name of all her family, that cup of wine which, under the name of the *loving cup*, has continued since the time of the Anglo-Saxons to form a part of all solemn public banquets.

A contagious disease at another time broke out in one part of his diocese, to which Cuthbert immediately betook himself. After having visited and consoled all the remaining inhabitants of one village, he turned to the priest who accompanied him, and asked, "Is there still any one sick in this poor place, whom I can bless before I depart?" "Then," says the priest, who has preserved this story to us, "I showed him in the distance a poor woman bathed in tears, one of whose sons was already dead, and who held the other in her arms, just about to render his last breath. The bishop rushed to her, and taking the dying child from its mother's arms, kissed it first, then blessed it, and restored it to the mother, saying to her, as the Son of God said to the widow of Nain, 'Woman, weep not; have no more fear or sorrow; your son is saved, and no more victims to this pestilence shall perish here.'"

No saint of his time or country had more frequent or affectionate intercourse than Cuthbert with the nuns, whose numbers and influence were daily increasing among the Anglo-Saxons, and especially in Northumberland. The greater part of them lived together in the great monasteries, such as Whitby and Coldingham, but some, especially those who were widows or of advanced age, lived in their own houses or with their relatives. Such was a woman devoted to the service of God, who had watched over Cuthbert's childhood (for he seems to have been early left an orphan), while he kept his sheep on the hills near Melrose, from the eighth year of his age until his entrance into the convent at the age of fifteen. He was tenderly grateful to her for her maternal care, and when he became a missionary, took advantage of every occasion furnished to him by his apostolic journeys to visit her whom he called his mother, in the village where she lived. On one occasion, when he was with her, a fire broke out in the village, and the flames, increased by a violent wind, threatened all the neighbouring roofs. "Fear nothing, dear mother," the young missionary said to her; "this fire will do you no harm;" and he began to pray. Suddenly the wind changed; the village was saved, and with it the thatched roof which sheltered the old age of her who had protected his infancy.

From the cottage of his foster-mother he went to the palaces of queens. The noble queen of Northumberland,

Etheldreda, the saint and virgin, had a great friendship for Cuthbert. She overwhelmed him and his monastery with gifts from her possessions, and wishing, besides, to offer him a personal token of her close affection, she embroidered for him, with her hands (for she embroidered beautifully), a stole and maniple covered with gold and precious stones. She chose to give him such a present that he might wear this memorial of her only in the presence of God, whom they both served, and accordingly would be obliged to keep her always in mind at the holy sacrifice.

Cuthbert was on still more intimate terms with the holy princesses, who, placed at the head of great communities of nuns, and sometimes even of monks, exercised so powerful an influence upon the Anglo-Saxon race, and particularly on Northumbria. While he was still at Melrose, the increasing fame of his sanctity and eloquence brought him often into the presence of the sister of king Oswy, who then reigned over the two Northumbrian kingdoms. This princess, Ebba, was abbess of the double monastery of Coldingham, the farthest north of all the religious establishments of Northumbria. Cuthbert was the guest for several days of the royal abbess, but he did not intermit on this occasion his pious exercises, nor, above all, his austerities and long prayers by night on the sea-shore.

To the end of his life he maintained a very intimate and constant friendship with another abbess of the blood-royal of Northumbria, Elfleda, niece of S. Oswald, and of king Oswy, who, though still quite young, exercised an influence much greater than that of Ebba upon the men and the events of her time. She had the liveliest affection for the prior of Lindisfarne, and at the same time an absolute confidence in his sanctity. When she was assailed by an alarming illness, which fell into paralysis, and found no remedy from physicians, she cried, "Ah! had I but something which belonged to my dear Cuthbert, I am sure I should be cured." A short time after, her friend sent her a linen girdle, which she hastened to put on, and in three days she was healed.

Shortly before his death, and during his last pastoral visitation, Cuthbert went to see Elfleda in the neighbourhood of the great monastery of Whitby, to consecrate a church which she had built there, and to converse with her for the last time. They dined together, and during the meal, seeing his knife drop from his trembling hand in the abstraction of supernatural thoughts, she had a last opportunity of admiring his prophetic intuition, and his constant care for the salvation of souls. The fatigue of the holy bishop, who said, laughingly, "I cannot eat all day long, you must give me a little rest"—the eagerness and pious curiosity of the young abbess, anxious to know and do everything, who rushes up breathless during the ceremony of the dedication to ask from the bishop a memento for a monk whose death she had just heard of—all these details form a picture complete in its simplicity, upon which the charmed mind can repose amid the savage habits and wild vicissitudes of the struggle, then more violent than ever, between the Northumbrians and the Picts, the Saxons and the Kelts.

But the last of all his visits was for another abbess less illustrious and less powerful than the two princesses of the blood, but also of high birth, and not less dear to his heart, if we may judge by the mark of affection which he gave her on his deathbed. This was Verca, abbess of one of that long line of monasteries which traced the shores of the Northern Sea. Her convent was on the mouth of the Tyne, the river which divided the two Northumbrian kingdoms. She gave Cuthbert a magnificent reception; but the bishop was ill, and after the mid-day meal, which was usual in all the Benedictine monasteries, he became thirsty. Wine and beer were offered to him, yet he would take nothing but water, but this water, after it had touched his lips, seemed to the monks of Tynemouth, who drank the remainder, the best wine they had ever tasted. Cuthbert, who retained nothing of the robust health of his youth, already suffered from the first attacks of the disease which carried him off. His pious friend was no doubt struck by his feebleness, for she offered him, as the last pledge ot spiritual union, a piece of very fine linen to be his shroud. Two short years of the episcopate had sufficed to consume his strength.

After celebrating the feast of Christmas, in 686, with the monks of Lindisfarne, the presentiment of approaching death determined him to abdicate, and to return to his isle of Farne, there to prepare for the last struggle. He lived but two months, in the dear and pleasant solitude which was his supreme joy, tempering its sweetness by redoubled austerities. When his monks came to visit him in his isle, which storms often made inaccessible for weeks together, they found him thin, tremulous, and almost exhausted. One of them, who has given us a narrative of the end of his life, revived him a little by giving him warm wine to drink, then seating himself by the side of the worn-out bishop upon his bed of stone, to sustain him, received from his beloved lips the last confidences and last exhortations of the venerated master. The visits of his monks were very sweet to him, and he lavished upon them to the last moment proofs of his paternal tenderness and of his minute care for their spiritual and temporal well-being. His last illness was long and painful. He fixed beforehand the place of his burial, near the oratory which he had hollowed in the rock, and at the foot of a cross which he had himself planted. "I would fain repose," said he, "in this spot, where I have fought my little battle for the Lord, where I desire to finish my course, and from whence I hope that my merciful Judge will call me to the crown of righteousness. You will bury me, wrapped in the linen which I have kept for my shroud, out of love for the abbess Verca, the friend of God, who gave it to me."

He ended his holy life preaching peace, humility, and the love of that unity which he thought he had succeeded in establishing in the great Anglo-Keltic sanctuary, the new abbot of which, Herefrid, begged of him a last message as a legacy to his community. "Be unanimous in your counsels," the dying bishop said to him in his faint voice; "live in good accord with the other servants of Christ; despise none of the faithful who ask your hospitality; treat them with friendly familiarity, not esteeming yourself better than others, who have the same faith, and often the same life. But have no communion with those who withdraw from the unity of Catholic peace, either by the illegal celebration of Easter, or by practical ill-doing. Remember always, if you must make a choice, that I infinitely prefer that you should leave this place, carrying my bones with you, rather than that you should remain here bent under the yoke of wicked heresy. Learn, and observe with diligence, the Catholic decrees of the fathers, and also the rules of monastic life which God has deigned to give you by my hands. I know that many have despised me in my life, but after my death you will see that my doctrine has not been despicable."

This effort was the last. He lost the power of speech, received the last sacraments in silence, and died raising his eyes and arms to heaven, at the hour when it was usual to sing matins, in the night of the 20th of March, 687. One of his attendants immediately mounted to the summit of the rock, where the lighthouse is now placed, and gave to the monks of Lindisfarne, by waving a lighted torch, the signal agreed upon to announce the death of the greatest saint who has given glory to that famous isle. He was but fifty, and had worn the monastic habit for thirty-five years.

Among many friends, he had one who was at once his oldest and most beloved, a priest called Herbert, who lived as an anchorite in an island of Lake Derwentwater. Every year Herbert came from his peaceful lake to visit his friend in the other island, beaten and undermined continually by the great waves of the Northern Sea; and upon that wild rock, to the accompaniment of winds and waves, they passed several days together, in a tender solitude and intimacy, talking of the life to come. When Cuthbert, then a bishop, came for the last time to Carlisle, Herbert seized the opportunity, and hastened to refresh himself at that fountain of eternal benefits which flowed for him from the holy and tender heart of his friend. "My brother," the bishop said to him, "thou must ask me now all that thou wantest to know, for we shall never meet again in this world." At these words Herbert fell at his feet in tears. "I conjure thee," he cried, "do not leave me on this earth behind thee; remember my faithful friendship, and pray God that, after having served Him together in this world, we may pass into His glory together." Cuthbert threw himself on his knees at his friend's side, and after praying for some minutes, said to him, "Rise, my brother, and weep no more; God has granted to us that which we have both asked from Him." And, in fact, though they never saw each other again here below, they died on the same day and at the same hour; the one in his isle bathed by the peaceful waters of a solitary lake, the other upon his granite rock, fringed by the ocean foam; and their souls, says Bede, reunited by that blessed death, were carried together by the angels into the eternal kingdom. This coincidence deeply touched the Christians of Northumbria, and was long engraven in their memory. Seven centuries later, in 1374, the bishop of

Carlisle appointed that a mass should be said on the anniversary of the two saints, in the island where the Cumbrian anchorite died, and granted an indulgence of forty days to all who crossed the water to pray there in honour of the two friends.

After many translations, the body of S. Cuthbert found repose in Durham cathedral, where it rested in a magnificent shrine till the reign of Henry VIII., when the royal commissioners visited the cathedral with the purpose of demolishing all shrines. The following is a condensed account of this horrible profanation, given by a writer of the period, or shortly after[1] :—

"The sacred shrine of holy S. Cuthbert was defaced at the visitation held at Durham, by Dr. Lee, Dr. Henly, and Mr. Blithman. They found many valuable jewels. After the spoil of his ornaments, they approached near to his body, expecting nothing but dust and ashes; but perceiving the chest he lay in strongly bound with iron, the goldsmith, with a smith's great forge hammer, broke it open, when they found him lying whole, uncorrupt, with his face bare, and his beard as of a fortnight's growth, and all the vestments about him, as he was accustomed to say mass. When the goldsmith perceived he had broken one of his legs in breaking open the chest, he was sore troubled at it, and cried, 'Alas! I have broken one of his legs'; which Dr. Henly hearing, called to him, and bade him cast down his bones. The other answered, he could not get them asunder, for the sinews and skin held them so that they would not separate. Then Dr. Lee stept up to see if it were so, and turning about, spake in Latin to Dr. Henly that he was entire, though Dr. Henly, not believing his words, called again to

[1] "A description or briefe declaration of all ye auntient monuments, &c., written in 1593," but this seems to have been written originally in Latin somewhat earlier. It has been several times republished, lastly by Sanderson, in 1767.

have his bones cast down. Dr. Lee answered, 'If you will not believe me, come up yourself and see him.' Then Dr. Henly stept up to him, and handled him, and found he lay whole; then he commanded them to take him down, and so it happened, that not only his body was whole and uncorrupted, but the vestments wherein his body lay, and wherein he was accustomed to say mass, were fresh, safe, and not consumed. Whereupon the visitors commanded him to be carried into the revestry, till the king's pleasure concerning him was further known; and upon the receipt thereof, the prior and monks buried him in the ground under the place where his shrine was exalted."

Harpsfield, who flourished at the time, and who was a most faithful and zealous Catholic, gives a similar account; he, however, does not say that the leg bone was broken, but that the flesh was wounded; and that the body was entire except that "the prominent part of the nose, I know not why, was wanting." And he adds that, "a grave was made in the ground, in that very spot previously occupied by his precious shrine, and there the body was deposited. And not only his body, but even the vestments in which it was clothed, were perfectly entire, and free from all taint and decay. There was upon his finger a ring of gold, ornamented with a sapphire, which I myself once saw and handled and kissed. There were present, among others, when this sacred body was exposed to daylight, Doctor Whithead, the president of the monastery, Dr. Sparke, Dr. Tod, and William Wilam, the keeper of the sacred shrine. And thus it is abundantly manifest, that the body of S. Cuthbert remained inviolate and uncontaminated eight hundred and forty years."

In May, 1827, the place which these and other authorities had indicated as that where the body of S. Cuthbert was buried, was very carefully examined, and the coffin and a body were exhumed. The Anglo-Saxon sculpture, and everything about and within this coffin, left no doubt that what was discovered was the ancient coffin, the vestments, and relics which had accompanied the body of S. Cuthbert. But the body by no means agreed with the minute accounts of S. Cuthbert. There was evidence that it had not been uncorrupt when buried, and there was no trace of any injury done to the leg-bone. Hence it is difficult not to conclude that the garments and shrine were those of Cuthbert, but that the body was *not his*, but was one which had been substituted for it. And when we remember that the incorrupt body was left in the vestry under the charge of the prior and monks till the king's pleasure could be ascertained as to what was to be done with it, there can be little doubt that they who so highly valued this sacred treasure substituted for it another body, which they laid in the pontifical vestments of Cuthbert, which was buried as his in his coffin. Where the prior and monks concealed the holy relics, if this conjecture prove true, it is impossible to state. That there is ground for this conjecture may be concluded from the existence of a tradition to this effect, and it is said that the true place of the interment of the saint is only known to three members of the Benedictine Order, who, as each one dies, choose a successor. Another line of tradition is said to descend through the Vicars Apostolic, now Roman Catholic bishops of the district. This is the belief to which reference is made in Marmion.

The supposed place of interment indicated by the secular tradition, (under the stairs of the bell-tower), has been carefully examined. No remains were found, and it is evident that the ground had never been disturbed since the construction of the tower.[1] There can be no question as to the

[1] This secular tradition was preserved in the following words :—" Subter gradus saxeos (secundum et tertium) climacis ascendentis et ducentis erga turrim campan-

genuineness of all the articles found in the tomb, for they exactly agree with accounts of the things contained in the shrine, described by pre-reformation writers; but the genuineness of the body is more than questionable. Mr. Raine, who was present at the investigation, and has written an account of it, "S. Cuthbert; with an Account of the State in which his Remains were found upon the Opening of his Tomb in Durham Cathedral, in the year 1827," Durham 1828, endeavours to establish their identity by repudiating as absurd the account of the contemporary writers who assert that the body was uncorrupt, and of the breaking of the leg-bone, though he accepts all their other statements.

arum in templo cathedrali civitatis Dunelmensis, prope horologium grande quod locatur in angulo australi fani ejusdem, sepultus jacet thesaurus pretiosus, (corpus S. Cuthberti.)" The earliest notice of such a tradition is in Serenus Cressy, (1688), Church History, p. 902. The next in two MSS. in Downside College by F. Mannock (1740), who states that he had heard it from F. Casse (1730.) Both these statements pointed to the removal of the body in the time of Henry VIII. The next notice of it is in 1828, when F. Gregory Robinson wrote to Lingard, (see Lingard's Remarks, p. 50), but in this account the removal was described as taking place in Mary's time. The secresy was partly broken when, in 1800, the sketch of the cathedral which exists in the archives of the Northern (R.C.) Province was allowed to be seen. Lingard's tradition (Anglo Saxon Church, ii. p. 80), about the exchange of S. Cuthbert's body for another skeleton is unknown to the Benedictines, who assert that they possess the secret. It is said that the Benedictine tradition concerning the site does not agree with the secular. What started the diggings in 1867, under the stairs, was that a hereditary Roman Catholic of Gateshead became a Protestant, and gave up a small piece of paper on which was written the above secular tradition, "*subter gradus, &c.*" His father or grandfather had been servant to a Vicar Apostolic, after whose death he had some of his clothes, among which was a waistcoat, inside which the above was secured. It was ascertained that this was not a hoax, and the late Dean Waddington invited some of the fathers from Ushaw over, and the head of the English Benedictines to see the diggings. It was supposed that the "precious treasure" was something else, perhaps the Black Rood of Scotland, containing a portion of the true cross, and that the words above in parenthesis, (corpus Sti. Cuthberti) are a gloss. However they dug, but found nothing but concrete and rock.

S. EADBERT, B. OF LINDISFARNE.

(A.D. 698.)

[Roman and Anglican Martyrologies. Some late Martyrologists, as Maurolycus, Canisius, Menardus, Bucelinus, &c., have confounded him with S. Egbert, who died at Iona, and who is commemorated on April 24th. Authority:—Bede's Eccl. Hist. iv. 29, 30, and his life of S. Cuthbert, c. 12.]

S. EADBERT is said to have been born amongst the South Saxons. He succeeded S. Cuthbert in the see of Lindisfarne, and Bede describes him as a man excelling in knowledge of the Holy Scriptures, and in observance of the angelic precepts. He administered the Church of Lindisfarne for about ten years; during which time it was his custom twice in the year—Advent and Lent—to make a retreat into the islet, where S. Cuthbert had resided, before he went to Farne. There he could be alone with God and his own soul, surrounded by the tumbling grey waves of the Northern ocean. He was present when the body of S. Cuthbert was translated, eleven years after the death of this great prelate, and the body was found perfectly fresh and incorrupt. Shortly after this event, Eadbert fell sick and died. He was placed in the sepulchre of S. Cuthbert.

S. ELFLEDA, V. ABSS. OF WHITBY.

(A.D. 716.)

[Inserted in Anglican Martyrology by J. Wilson, and in the Benedictine by Hugh Menard; and Ferrarius in his Gen. Catalogue. Authorities :—Bede and Malmesbury.]

THROUGHOUT his life, Penda, the fierce heathen king of Mercia, or the midland counties of England, waged war with the kingdom of Northumbria, which included Yorkshire, Durham, and Northumberland. But this bloodthirsty and stubborn hatred led him to his destruction. Oswy, son of Ethelfrid, the ravager, and grandson of Ida, the Man of Fire, was king of Northumbria, which had been so wasted and exhausted by the former ravages of Penda, that it could ill withstand another attack. It was only at the last extremity, that king Oswy resolved to engage in a final conflict with the terrible enemy who had conquered and slain his two predecessors, Edwin and the saintly Oswald. He had married his son and his daughter to children of Penda; and he gave him another of his sons as a hostage. But Penda would not consent to any durable peace. During the thirteen years that had elapsed since the overthrow of Oswald, and the accession of Oswy, he had periodically subjected Northumberland to frightful devastations. In vain Oswy, driven to desperation, offered him all his jewels, ornaments, and treasures, of which he could dispose, as a ransom for his desolated and hopeless provinces. The arrogant and fierce octogenarian refused everything, being resolute, as he said, to exterminate the whole Northumbrian race, from first to last. "Well, then," said Oswy, "since this heathen despises our gifts, let us offer them to one who will accept them—to the Lord our God." He then made a vow to devote to God a daughter who had just been born to him, and at the same time to give twelve estates for the foundation of as many monasteries. After this he marched at the head of a small army against Penda, whose troops were, according to a Northumbrian tradition, thirty times more numerous, and a battle was fought near the site of the present town of Leeds, in which Penda was defeated and slain. Thus perished, at the age of eighty, after a reign of thirty years, the conqueror and murderer of five Anglo-Saxon kings, and the last and indefatigable champion of paganism among the Anglo-Saxons.

Oswy faithfully kept his word. He set apart twelve estates to be thenceforward monastic property—six in the north, and six in the south of his double kingdom. He then took his daughter Elfleda, who was but yet a year old, and consecrated her to God by the vow of perpetual virginity. Her mother, the daughter of Edwin, first Christian king of Northumbria, had been also dedicated to God from her birth, but only by baptism, and as a token of the gratitude of a still pagan father for the protection of the Christian's God. The daughter of Oswy was to be the price of a yet higher gift of heaven—the conclusive victory of his race, and of the Christian faith in his country; the sacrifice reminds us of that of Jepthah's daughter; but she, far from desiring to escape her vow, showed herself, during a long life, always worthy of her heavenly Bridegroom. The king took her from the caresses of her mother, to intrust her to the abbess Hilda of Hartlepool, who nearly ten years before had been initiated into the monastic life by S. Aidan.

In 658, when Elfleda was three years old, S. Hilda founded her monastery of Streaneshalch, now called Whitby, and moved thither with her little spiritual daughter.

Elfleda was scarcely twenty-five years of age, when S. Hilda died, and she was called to succeed her as abbess of Whitby. She is described by Bede as a most pious mistress of spiritual life. But like all the Anglo-Saxon princesses whom we meet within the cloister at this epoch, she did not cease to take a passionate interest in the affairs of her race and her country, and to exercise that extraordinary and salutary influence which was so willingly yielded by the Anglo-Saxon kings and people to those princesses of their sovereign races who became the brides of Christ.

She maintained that reverent and affectionate relation with S. Cuthbert which had been maintained by S. Hilda.

Before he became bishop, while he lived on a desert rock near Lindisfarne, she prevailed on him to grant her an interview in an island on the Northumbrian coast, called then, as now, Coquet Island. She was anxious and alarmed for her brother Egfrid, and she desired to consult the holy Cuthbert on the affairs of the state and her family. The hermit and the abbess went each to their meeting by sea; and when he had answered all her questions, she threw herself at his feet, and entreated him to tell her, by virtue of those prophetic powers, with which he was known to be gifted, whether her brother, Egfrid, would have a long life and reign. "I am surprised," he answered, "that a woman well versed, like you, in the Holy Scriptures should speak to me of length with regard to human life, which lasts no longer than a spider's web, as the Psalmist has said. How short then must life be for a man who has but a year to live, and has death at his door!" At these words, she wept long; then, drying her tears, she continued, with feminine boldness, and inquired who should be the king's successor, since he had neither sons nor brothers. "Do not say," he replied, "that he is without heirs; he shall have a successor whom you will love, as you love Egfrid, as a sister." "Then tell me, I entreat you, where this successor is." "You see," returned Cuthbert, directing the eyes of his companion towards the archipelago of islets which dots the Northumbrian coast around Lindisfarne, "how many isles are in the vast ocean; it is easy for God to bring from them some one to reign over the English." Elfleda then perceived that he spoke of a young man, Aldfrid, supposed to be the son of her father Oswy, by an Irish mother, and who, since his infancy, had lived as an exile at Iona, where he gave himself up to study.

The troubles concerning S. Wilfrid which had vexed the Northumbrian Church still prevailed. Wilfrid was still in banishment for his persistence in introducing the Roman customs into the Keltic Church of the north of England. The new king, Aldfrid, had brought with him from Iona attachment to the ritual of SS. Columba and Aidan. Elfleda inherited the prejudices of her spiritual mother, Hilda, against the stern and inflexible innovator; but there was on their side a desire for reconcilation with the Church of the province of Canterbury, which was of Roman foundation, and they hoped that now Wilfrid was an aged man, some of his harshness might have been softened.

To the new king, as well as to his sister, the Abbess Elfleda, Archbishop Theodore of Canterbury wrote, to exhort them both to lay aside their enmity against Wilfrid, and to receive him with unreserved kindness. They yielded, and recalled Wilfrid, but were mistaken in supposing that age had altered his determination. He returned in 687 to excite storms throughout his diocese, and was again exiled, in 691.

Aldfrid died in 705, and the Northumbrian crown descended to a prince named Eadwulf. Wilfrid had taken advantage of the death of Aldfrid to return to Ripon, but was ordered to leave the country in six days. But Eadwulf was dethroned, and a son of Aldfrid, Osred, aged eight, was given the realm of Bernicia, the counties of Northumberland and Durham. By means of some mysterious influence, the nature of which is unknown, the aged exile Wilfrid, who had been expelled from the country for fourteen years, and was to all appearance forgotten, became, all at once, the master of the situation, and the arbiter of events. He soon acquired a more powerful protector than the young sovereign in the person of Earl Bertfrid, who was considered the most powerful noble in the kingdom, and who was at the head of Osred's party. King Eadwulf marched against the insurgents, and obliged them to retreat to the fortress of Bamborough, where the earl, shut up in the narrow enclosure of this fortified rock, and reduced to the last extremity, vowed that, if God would deliver him and his charge, the young prince and his people should bow to the Roman subjection. An opportune desertion of Eadwulf's followers gave victory to Bertfrid, and Eadwulf was exiled after a short reign of two months. As soon as the royal child was placed on the throne, the Archbishop of Canterbury made his appearance, perceiving that the time was come for reinstating Wilfrid, and settling his affairs in a general assembly. This was held in the open air on the banks of the Nid. Wilfrid was present, and met there Bertfrid and the Abbess Elfleda, who had come over to his side, and to Roman obedience. All the Northumbrians regarded her as the consoler and best counsellor of the kingdom. The bishops and abbots present opposed the claims of Wilfrid, and refused to accept him, though he came armed with the authority of the Holy See. At this point, the Abbess Elfleda interposed: in a voice which all listened to as an utterance from heaven, she described the last illness and agony of the king her brother, and how he had vowed to God and S. Peter to accomplish the papal decrees which he had so vigorously rejected. "This," she said, "is the last will of Aldfrid the king; I attest the truth of it before Christ." Bertfrid afterwards spoke and announced his vow. Nevertheless the three bishops would not yield, they retired from the assembly to confer among themselves, and with Archbishop Britwald, but above all with the sagacious Elfleda. Thanks to her, all ended in a general reconciliation.

Shortly before his death, and during his last pastoral visitation, S. Cuthbert went to see Elfleda in the neighbourhood of the great monastery of Whitby, to consecrate a church which she had built there, and to converse with her for the last time. They dined together, and during the meal, seeing his knife drop from his trembling hand in the abstraction of supernatural thoughts, she had a last opportunity of admiring his prophetic intuition, and his constant care for the salvation of souls. The fatigue of the holy bishop, who said laughingly, "I cannot eat all day long; you must give me a little rest": The eagerness and pious curiosity of the young abbess, anxious to know and do everything, who rushed up breathlessly during the ceremony of the dedication to ask the bishop a *memento* for a monk, whose death she had just heard of,—all these details, says a modern writer,[1] form a picture complete

[1] Montalembert, Monks of the West, iv. p. 412.

in its simplicity, upon which the charmed mind can repose amid the savage habits and wild vicissitudes of the struggle, then more violent than ever, between the Northumbrians and Picts, the Saxons and the Celts.

S. Elfleda died at the age of sixty. No account of her last illness has been transmitted to us.

S. JOHN OF BEVERLEY, ABP.

(A.D. 721.)

[Roman and Anglican Martyrologies. York and Sarum Kalendars, October 28th, as the day of his Translation. Authority:—A life by Folcard, monk of Canterbury (fl. 1066), at the request of Aldred, Arch bishop of York; too late to contain much that is life-like and of great interest. Bede also mentions S. John in several places. Bede is an excellent authority, for he was a pupil of S. John, and was ordained by him.]

S. John was educated at the famous school of S. Theodore, Archbishop of Canterbury, under the holy abbot Adrian (January 9th.) On his return to the North of England, his native country, he entered the monastery of Whitby, governed by the abbess Hilda. On the death of Eata, he was appointed and consecrated to the bishopric of Hagulstad, or Hexham, by Archbishop Theodore. When S. Wilfred was recalled from banishment in 686, by Aldfrid, King of Northumbria, all the bishops appointed by Archbishop Theodore in the province of York, viz., three, Hexham, Ripon, and York, were displaced. S. Cuthbert voluntarily resigned his see of Lindisfarne, and for a brief space S. Wilfred recovered what he considered to be his rights. But the restoration lasted only a year, and Wilfred was again driven into banishment. Probably S. John then resumed the government of the see of Hexham. But this is uncertain. On the death of Wilfred, Bosa was appointed to the see of York, and when Bosa died, John was chosen to fill the see.

He founded the monastery of Beverley, in the midst of the wood then called Deirwald, or the Forest of Deira, among the ruins of the deserted Roman settlement of Petuaria. This monastery, like so many others of the Anglo-Saxons, was a double community of monks and nuns. In 717, broken with age and fatigue, S. John ordained his chaplain, Wilfred the Younger, and having appointed him to govern the see of York, retired for the remaining years of his life to Beverley, where he died in 721.

S. ETHELWOLD, H.

(ABOUT A.D. 723.)

[Menardus on Jan. 6th. Edward Mayhew in his Trophæa Cong. Anglic. O.S.B. on March 23rd. So Heronymus Porter in his Flores Vitarum Sanct. Angliæ, Scotiæ, and Hiberniæ. The revised Anglican Martyrology of 1640, on same day. Authority:—Bede in his life of S. Cuthbert.]

S. ETHETWOLD, or ETHELWOLD, was for some time a monk at Ripon, "where having received the priestly office," says Bede, "he sanctified it by a life worthy of that degree. After the death of that man of God, Cuthbert, this venerable priest succeeded him in the exercise of a solitary life, in the cell which the saint had inhabited in the islet of Farne, before he was made bishop." He found the oratory of Cuthbert so rudely put together, that the sea-wind shrieked in through the joints of the planks, and though patched up with clay and stubble, the chapel was so full of draughts that Ethelwold asked for and obtained a calf's skin, and this he nailed against the wall where he was wont to pray, to keep the wind from blowing into his ear. Bede says, "I will relate one miracle of Ethelwold, which was told me by one of the brothers who was concerned, and for whose sake it was wrought, Guthfried, the venerable servant and priest of Christ, who afterwards presided in quality of abbot over the church of Lindisfarne, in which he was educated. I came, said he, to the islet of Farne, with two other brothers, desiring to speak with the most reverent father Ethelwold; and when we had been comforted by his discourses, and having asked his blessing, were returning home, when on a sudden, as we were in the sea, the fair weather that was wafting us over changed, and so great and furious a storm fell on us, that neither sail nor oars availed, and we despaired of life.

"Having a good while struggled in vain with the wind and waves, we looked back at last to see if by any means we might return to the island, but found that we were equally beset with the tempest on all sides; but we could perceive Ethelwold at the mouth of his cavern, contemplating our danger. For, hearing the howl of the wind, and the roar of the sea, he came forth to see how we fared. And when he saw our desperate condition, he bent his knees to the Father of our Lord Jesus Christ, to pray for our life and safety. As he finished his prayer, the swelling sea immediately abated its violence, and the rage of the winds ceased, and a fair gale springing up bore us over the smooth waters to the shore. But no sooner had we arrived, and drawn our boat out of the water, than the same storm began to rage again, and ceased not all that day; to the end that it might plainly appear, that this small intermission had been granted from heaven at the prayer of the man of God, that we might escape."

S. Ethelwold spent twelve years at Farne, and died there; but he was buried in Lindisfarne, in the Church of S. Peter, near the bodies of SS. Cuthbert and Eadbert. His bones were afterwards taken up in the time of the Danish ravages, 875, and were translated to Durham in 995, and more honourably enshrined in 1160.

S. CEOLWULF, K., MONK.

(A.D. 767.)

[Old English Martyrologies on March 14th; later ones on this day, on which he is commemorated in the Roman Calendar. Authorities: Bede, Florence of Worcester, William of Malmesbury, Henry Huntingdon, Simeon of Durham, &c.]

Bede dedicated his "History of the English" to Ceolwulf, King of Northumbria, whose tender solicitude for monastic interests made the monk of Jarrow look to him as a patron. Ceolwulf was of the race of Ida the Burner; after two obscure reigns, Ceolwulf was called to the throne, and vainly attempted to struggle against the disorder and decay of his country. He was vanquished and made captive by enemies whose names are not recorded, and was shut up in a convent. He escaped, however, regained the crown, and reigned for some time in a manner which gained the applause of Bede. But after a reign of eight years, a regret, or an unconquerable desire for that monastic life which had been formerly forced upon him against his will, seized him. He made the best provisions possible for the security of his country, and for a good understanding between the spiritual and temporal authorities, nominating as his successor a worthy prince of his race. Then, giving up the cares of power, and showing himself truly the master of the wealth he resigned, he cut his long beard, had his head shaved in the form of a crown, and retired to bury himself anew in the holy island of Lindisfarne, in the monastery beaten by the winds and waves of the northern sea. There he passed the last thirty years of his life in study and happiness. He had, while king, enriched this monastery with many great gifts, and obtained permission for the use of wine and beer for the monks, who, up to that time, according to the rigid rule of ancient Keltic discipline, had been allowed no beverage but water and milk.

S. JOHN OF BEVERLEY, ABP. OF YORK.

B. ALCUIN, P. MK.

(A.D. 804.)

[Gallican Martyrologies. Hrabanus, Greven and Molanus in their additions to Usuardus. Authority :—A life by a writer almost his contemporary, and his own writings. The life was written before 829, according to Sigulf the disciple of Alcuin, who furnished the writer with much of his information. But this life is colourless and poor. Far richer details may be gathered from the epistles of Alcuin. A good modern life of Alcuin is that of Dr. F. Lorenz, professor of history to the University of Halle.]

THE last of the distinguished Anglo-Saxons whose name shed lustre on the empire of the Frankish monarchs in the eighth century, was Alcuin. Born at York, about the year 735, of a noble family, Alcuin [1] was scarcely weaned from his mother's breast when he was dedicated to the Church, and entrusted to the care of the inmates of a monastery, and on reaching the proper age, he was placed in the school of Archbishop Egbert, then celebrated for the number of noble youths who crowded thither to imbibe instruction from the lips of that saintly prelate. Alcuin was distinguished above his fellows by his application to the study of the sciences, which were taught by Egbert's kinsman Aelbert, who succeeded him in 766 in the see of York, and in the management of the school. Alcuin was Aelbert's favourite pupil; when about twenty years of age, he was chosen to accompany him on a visit to the conti-

[1] His name was originally Albeis, why and when he changed it does not appear.

nent in search of books, and of new discoveries in science, and on that occasion he resided for a short time in Rome. Immediately after Aelbert's accession to the archiepiscopal see, he ordained Alcuin deacon, appointed him to fill the place which he had himself occupied in the school, and gave him the care of the extensive library attached to it. Under Alcuin's superintendence the school increased in reputation, and many foreigners came to partake of the advantages derived from his teaching. Archbishop Aelbert died on the 8th November, 780, and was succeeded by Eanbald, one of Alcuin's pupils, who, in the following year, sent his instructor to Rome to obtain for him the pall at the hands of Pope Adrian I. On his return, Alcuin visited Parma, and there met Charlemagne, who had also been at Rome. That monarch was then meditating the foundation of scholastic institutions throughout his dominions, and he seized the opportunity to persuade Alcuin to settle in France, and become his adviser and assistant in his projects of reform.

There must have been something peculiarly engaging in Charlemagne. Alcuin met a great mind, full of noble aspirations, in advance of his age, and he saw that the emperor was a man whom he might direct aright, and who was one to render him every facility for raising the religious, moral and intellectual tone of the mighty empire over which Charlemagne had been placed. But before he joined the king, Alcuin continued his journey home, to fulfil his original commission, and to obtain the consent of the archbishop of York, and of Alfwold, king of Northumbria, to the proposed arrangement. He felt, and so did his spiritual and temporal superiors, that a door had been opened before him, and that it was not for them to attempt to close it. In 782, followed by some of his chosen disciples, Alcuin left England for France. In the court of Charlemagne, Alcuin became, as one great writer[1] calls him, the intellectual prime minister of the emperor.

A slight sketch of the condition of the Church in the empire is necessary, that the reader may judge of the abuses Charlemagne and Alcuin had united to rectify.

The higher classes of the clergy under the Franks at the time of the Merovingian princes were, according to the testimony of their contemporary and fellow-clerk, Gregory of Tours, to the last extent barbarous, dissolute, and corrupt. Adultery, murder, simony, false swearing, avarice, abounded among the bishops and dignitaries, and the example of the higher clergy corrupted those below them, and demoralized the laity.

The episcopal thrones in Germany were occupied by Franks, and when S. Boniface came in the eighth century into Germany to convert the heathen, he found occasion to vehemently inveigh against the morals and conduct of the German bishops. His account of the Frankish clergy gives a terrible picture of disorder. He wrote to Pope Zacharias: "For long religion has been prostrate. In the course of eighty years the Franks have not held a single council, nor published a new decree, nor renewed a single old one. The possessors of the bishoprics are avaricious laymen, or adulterous priests, who only aim at temporal profit. Their deacons live from youth up in adultery and all uncleanness, and whilst still deacons have as many as four or five concubines. Nevertheless they are so bold that they read the Gospel publicly, and are not ashamed to style themselves deacons. If they attain the priestly office, laden with all their crimes, they lead the same criminal life, heap one sin upon another, and yet pretend to intercede for the people, and offer the Holy Sacrifice. The worst is that these men advance from one dignity to

[1] Agobard, Archbishop of Lyons.

another, and finally become bishops. If there are any among them who remain chaste, yet they give themselves up to drinking, hunting, and injustice, or go armed to battle, and shed with their own hands human blood, sometimes that of heathen, but sometimes also that of Christians."

Bishop Gewilieb, of Mayence, was charged by S. Boniface with murder, before a council at Worms, because he had killed in duel a Saxon who had assassinated his father, Bishop Gerold of Worms. S. Boniface also charged Bishop Gewilieb with being addicted to hawking and hunting, and endeavoured to obtain his deposition.

The cause of the decay of discipline and general disorder in morals was probably this. The Frank kings saw how much their power would be supported and strengthened if the widely ramifying authority of the Church were made a base for their throne. They therefore richly endowed bishoprics and abbeys, and made the bishops and abbots to be vassals (*ministrales*) of the king. Thus Fredegar, in 740, speaks of the Burgundian barons, whether bishops or other feudatories.[1] They were often employed in affairs of the State, and were thus invested with a very important political influence. The possessions of the Church were regarded by the kings as feudal tenures (*beneficia*), and the bishops and abbots holding them were bound to arm and fight as vassals for their king. It was stipulated by law that the choice of a bishop should be confirmed by the king;[2] but for the most part, the kings themselves appointed to the vacant sees, in spite of the often reiterated protests of the councils. Synods could not assemble without the royal permission; their decrees had to be confirmed by the king, being previously invalid. In the meantime the affairs of the Church were discussed and ordered, even

[1] Fredigar, Chron., caps. 4, 76.

[2] Conc. Aurelian, ann. 849.

in the meetings of the king's council of Vassals, the *placitum regis, synodus regia;* and the government of ecclesiastical affairs having thus passed into the hands of the State, synods of bishops and clergy became more rare, and at length ceased altogether. This arrangement completed the downfall of the metropolitan system. The king became the sole and sovereign judge of the bishops. "If one of us, O King," wrote Gregory of Tours to King Chilperic, "shall have wished to transgress the path of justice, he is judged by thee, but if thou transgressest, who is to call thee to order? We may speak to thee, and if it pleases thee, thou mayest attend; but if thou willest not to listen, who is to condemn thee, except He Who is very Justice?"[1]

In proportion as the bishops rose higher in political influence, the other clergy sank deeper. No free man was allowed to receive orders without royal permission. Hence the clergy were chosen for the most part from among the serfs, and on this very account the bishops acquired an unlimited power over them, which frequently manifested itself in the most tyrannical conduct.

S. Boniface found the German Church in this deplorable condition; bishops and abbots mere creatures of the State, wealthy, and sometimes not even in holy orders, but enjoying the temporalities without a thought of qualifying to administer the spiritualities of their charge. He strove to bring the bishops from this servitude to the crown into responsibility to the pope, hoping thereby to check the evil. But this could not be done without an alteration in the law. The abbots and bishops who held many feudal tenures were bound by a law of Charles Martel to march to war at the head of their retainers; they were often engaged for a long period in fighting, and their abode in the camp

[1] Hist. Franc., v. 19.

speedily assimilated them in morals and sentiments to the other feudal lords. For the extension of Christianity, the first missionaries had established numerous monastic colonies throughout Germany, and these were supported by the agricultural labours ofthe m onks. But by degrees the farming interest prevailed over the spiritual in these houses. The monks proved themselves admirable agriculturists, and for the sake of the cultivation of their fields neglected the harvest of souls. When Charlemagne ascended the throne, he found the Frank and German episcopal thrones and abbots' chairs occupied by men without learning and without morals, fighting, drinking, hunting, and utterly neglectful of their spiritual calling. Charlemagne was resolved to raise the people committed to his charge from the chains of ignorance and barbarism which held them fast. To effect this he must begin by correcting the evil in head-quarters. He cut off the chief occasion of evil by exempting the bishops and abbots from military service, and he forbade them to hunt with hawks and hounds in the forests. This latter regulation, though repeatedly formulated, he found it impossible to enforce. The prelates were ready enough to be exempt from war, which broke in on their ease, but the chase was to them a darling pleasure of which they would not be deprived. At length Charlemagne, finding it impracticable to enforce his rule, and unwilling to acknowledge the impracticability, by law permitted the higher clergy to hunt, on condition that the skins of the beasts killed were used for binding books.

This reminds us of a story told of Charlemagne which we should be sorry to suppose is fabulous. He was one day hunting in a forest, and lost his way. As night fell he came to a little church and priest's house, and asked for a lodging. It was readily accorded him, but his fare was scanty, though the best the poor priest could offer. On the morrow the priest made the emperor hear mass, which he celebrated very devoutly, and then gave his guest, of whose rank he was ignorant, a plain breakfast, and dismissed him with his blessing. The emperor, pleased with his piety, and compassionating the poverty of his host, offered him a piece of gold, which the priest refused, saying, "Sir, I need not thy money, but if thou killest a hind to-day, I pray thee give me the skin, for my old Breviary sadly needs a cover." Charlemagne, ever ready to advance good men, did not forget the poor priest in the forest, but on the see of Trèves falling vacant, appointed to it his host of that night. If this story rests on a true foundation, the priest was Amalarius, who afterwards as archbishop became a confidential adviser of the emperor.

Charlemagne, under the direction of Alcuin, founded schools in which young clerics could be educated and disciplined, to shine as lights in the world, and not become a scandal to Christendom like the clergy under his predecessors. By the determination and zeal of the emperor and Alcuin, the sees were one after another filled with worthy bishops, men of learning and piety, and Charlemagne was able to entrust to them the execution of justice in matters temporal within their dioceses as well as spiritual government. He also chose from among them extraordinary judges (*Missi dominici*) whom he sent round every year into every province to exercise the highest oversight and power in things ecclesiastical as well as civil. With every bishop thus appointed was also a count. Bishops and counts were everywhere instructed to work together, and mutually to support one another; ecclesiastical usurpations were not endured,[1] and the oppressions of the counts and dukes weighing on the people were removed.

In addition to these duties, the bishops were required to

[1] See Capitulars for A.D. 779 (Baluz., i., 197, 387.)

sentence for his crimes from Bishop Theodulf escaped from prison, and fled to Tours, where he took refuge in the sanctuary of S. Martin's abbey. Theodulf reclaimed the runaway; the monks of S. Martin's vehemently maintained their privilege of sanctuary, and armed their retainers against the officers of the bishop. All this took place without the knowledge of Alcuin, who was abbot of S. Martin's, but when he did hear of it he took the side of his monks, and refused to deliver up the culprit to the imperial officer sent by orders of Charlemagne to claim him. Alcuin wrote to the emperor a vehement letter maintaining the rights of the sanctuary; but Charlemagne earnestly deprecated the warmth and opposition of his bosom friend and preceptor, and insisted on the surrender of the culprit. This firmness no doubt cost him a pang, and it hastened Alcuin's death, but it shows that Charlemagne preferred justice to every other consideration.

A great improvement was also wrought by Charlemagne and Alcuin in the condition of the monks. To wean them from absorption in agricultural pursuits, they laboured to impress on them the importance of learning, and by appointing to the monasteries abbots who had been trained in the schools founded and watched over by Alcuin, an impulse was given to learning which made the monasteries of S. Gall, Fulda, and in later times Corbey and others, famous nurseries of science and book knowledge.

But to return to the main outline of the life of this great instigator of all the reforms wrought by Charlemagne, whose influence on the condition of the Church in that and the succeeding reigns can hardly be over estimated.

It is probable that Alcuin attended Charlemagne in many of his expeditions; he lost no opportunity in making his influence with the king subservient to the interests of his native country; and after remaining about eight years in France, he resolved to return to York. Charlemagne exacted from him a promise that he would return speedily, and make the court of France his lasting home; a promise Alcuin was not unwilling to give, for he saw that God had given him a mighty work to accomplish, and that he dare not withdraw from it.

"Although," said he, "I possess no small inheritance in my own country, I will willingly resign it, and in poverty serve thee, and remain with thee; let it be thy care to obtain the permission of my king and my bishop."

Alcuin came to England in the year 790, as ambassador from Charlemagne to King Offa, to arrange some misunderstanding which had arisen between the two great monarchs, and it appears to have been his intention to return the same year. But he found the kingdom of Northumbria involved in troubles; and in a letter written at this period, he laments that he should not be able to return to France at the time he expected. It was not till 792 that, pressed by the letters of Charlemagne, who desired his assistance in repressing a heresy which threatened to cause a division in the Frank Church, Alcuin left England for the last time, with the permission of Bishop Eanbald and King Ethelred. He took with him a number of English ecclesiastics, who were afterwards present at the council held in 794, at Frankfort-on-the Maïne, where the doctrinal innovations of Felix of Urgel and Elipandus of Toledo, who taught that Christ was the Son of God by adoption, were condemned. From 792 to 796 Alcuin continued to reside at the court of Charlemagne, in the same relation to his patron as before his visit to England. His position was rendered agreeable not only by the favour of the royal family, but by being in the society of the most learned and enlightened men of his time. Yet his happiness was frequently clouded by grief at the troubles with which his native country was visited, and of which he heard from his Northumbrian friends. In 793, the Norsemen devastated the island of Lindisfarne, profaned its church, and murdered several of the monks. This calamity, which Alcuin made the subject of one of the best of his poems, is alluded to in several of his letters, and appears to have afforded him keen distress, as well it might, for Lindisfarne was the ancient Christian metropolis of the North of England, endeared by the memory of S. Cuthbert, S. Aidan, and many another illustrious saint.

During the years which preceded A.D. 796, Charlemagne had been occupied in wars against the Saxons and Huns, and in that year, having reduced both these nations to his obedience, his mind was occupied with measures for the propagation of Christianity among the latter people. He consulted Alcuin, who, in an interesting letter, congratulated him on his conquests, and advised him to proceed with mildness rather than harshness in the work of conversion. Alcuin's liberality of sentiment is remarkably conspicuous in this letter; he recommends the king in the first place to select with care the missionaries whom he is about to send amongst them, and to avoid burdening the converts by the imposition of heavy rates for the support of the Church. He warns him against the immediate exaction of tithes, and entreats him to consider that a tax which established Christians reluctantly consented to pay, would prove intolerable to new converts, and might embitter the people against the religion of Christ.

The correspondence of Alcuin during the year 796 is unusually interesting, and exhibits his intelligent mind in a new light. Among the scholars at the court of Charlemagne it was a custom, not unknown in other times, of taking literary names and surnames. In this learned nomenclature Alcuin himself took the name of Flaccus Albinus, which in after ages was frequently appended to his writings; the common name whereby Charlemagne was designated was David; among Alcuin's more immediate friends, Riculf, archbishop of Mainz, was addressed as Damoetas; the name of Arno was changed into Aquila, and to Angilbert was given the name of Homer.

At last, at the age of sixty, Alcuin resolved to leave the court, and spend the rest of his days in seclusion. He determined to return to his native country, and repose for the remainder of his life in the cloister of the monastery of York. He had already made preparations for his departure, and was entrusted with rich presents for King Offa, when the intelligence of new troubles in the kingdom of Northumbria, and of the murder of King Ethelred, diverted him from his project. "I was prepared with gifts of King Charles to visit you, and to return to my country," he wrote to Offa; "but I have thought it better on account of the peace of my people to remain in pilgrimage, not knowing what I should do amongst those with whom no one can be secure, and who cannot profit by healthful counsel."

From this moment Alcuin resolved to spend the remainder of his life in the Frankish empire; but persisting in his intention of living in solitude, he demanded the permission of his royal patron to retire to Fulda. Charles was unwilling to lose the society of his favourite instructor and adviser, and refused his consent; but shortly afterwards he gave him the abbey of S. Martin, at Tours, which had become vacant by the opportune death of the abbot Itherius, with permission to spend as much of his time as he liked within the walls of that monastic house. Alcuin's mode of life at Tours was one rather of splendid retirement than of pure renunciation of the world. His theological opponent, Elipandus, blamed him for his enormous wealth. Though he seldom quitted his monastery, he continued still to be the favourite counsellor of the king, who in cases of emergency went to consult him at Tours. The monastic school which Alcuin established there, produced some of the most remarkable scholars of the following age. He sent a mission to England to procure books for its library, and it was there that he composed most of his writings.

In 803 the quarrel between himself and Bishop Theodulf of Orleans, already mentioned, led to a temporary estrangement between himself and Charlemagne.

Alcuin died at Tours, on Whit-Sunday, the 19th of May, 804, and was buried with great pomp in the church of S. Martin. In the Lyceum at Bamberg is preserved a Bible written by the hand of Alcuin for Charlemagne.

S. OSWALD, ARCHB. OF YORK.

(A.D. 992.)

[Wilson's Anglican Martyrology, and those of Wyon, Menardus, and Morolycus. But Molanus on October 15th. Authorities :—His life by Eadmer; also Florence of Worcester, William of Malmesbury, and the Ramsey Chronicle.]

OSWALD, the only saint commemorated on Feb. 29th, was the nephew of S. Odo, archbishop of Canterbury, and of Osketill, bishop, first of Dorchester, and afterwards of York. He was educated by S. Odo, and made first canon and then dean of Winchester, but he took the monastic habit in the abbey of Fleury, in France, and was re-called by S. Odo to England, where he found favour with S. Dunstan, who commended him to king Edgar, and, by his command, he was chosen bishop of Worcester, about the year 959. One of his first acts was to establish twelve monks at Westbury, in his diocese. He afterwards built Ramsey monastery, on an island in Ramsey Mere, given to the Order of S. Benedict by Earl Hilwyn, cousin of king Edgar, who had been cured of gout by an apparition of the patriarch of western monks. S. Dunstan, as is well known, laboured diligently to enforce celibacy on the clergy in England. A council was held in 969, in which the clergy were ordered to live single or to resign their cures, and Oswald of Worcester, and Ethelwold of Winchester, were commissioned to enforce this decree. Oswald was afterwards made archbishop of York, without resigning the see of Worcester.

He had established a Benedictine monastery, dedicated to the Mother of God, at Worcester, and the monastic church from that time became the Cathedral.

It was his wont to wash every day the feet of twelve poor men, whom he afterwards fed. On the Tuesday after the third Sunday in Lent, Feb. 29th, he was performing this duty as usual. After he had wiped the feet of the last poor man, and had stooped to kiss them, he said "Glory be to the Father, and to the Son, and to the Holy Ghost," and gently expired.

He died, and was buried at Worcester. Ten years after, his remains were taken up by his successor, Adulph, and translated to York, on October 15th. It is said that when his body was taken into Worcester Abbey Church, after his death, a white dove hovered above it. His purple and gold stole was preserved in Beverley Minster, in the time of Thomas Stubbs, who mentions the fact in his account of the Archbishops of York.

S. AELRED, ABBOT OF RIEVAUX.
From a Design by A. Welby Pugin.

S. AELRED, AB. OF RIEVAULX.

(A.D. 1166.)

[Authorities : His life in Capgrave, and his own writings, still extant.]

He was of noble descent, and was born in the north of England, in 1109. Being educated in learning and piety, he was invited by David, the pious King of Scotland, to his court, made master of his household, and highly esteemed both by him and the courtiers. His virtue shone with bright lustre in the world, particularly his meekness, which Christ declared to be his favourite virtue, and the distinguishing mark of his true disciples. The following is a memorable instance to what a degree S. Aelred possessed this virtue :—A certain person of quality having insulted and reproached him in the presence of the King, Aelred heard him out with patience, and thanked him for his charity and sincerity, in telling him his faults. This behaviour had such an influence on his adversary that it made him ask his pardon on the spot. Another time, whilst he was speaking on a certain matter, one interrupted him with very harsh reviling expressions : the servant of God heard him with tranquility, and afterward resumed his discourse with the same calmness and presence of mind as before. He desired ardently to devote himself entirely to God, by forsaking the world ; but the charms of friendship detained him some time longer in it, and were fetters to his soul ; reflecting notwithstanding that he must sooner or later be separated by death from those he loved most, he condemned his own cowardice, and broke at once those bands of friendship, which were more agreeable to him than all other sweets of life. To relinquish entirely all his worldly engagements, he left Scotland, and embraced the austere Cistercian order, at Rievaulx, in Yorkshire, where Walter de l'Especke had founded a monastery in 1122. At the age of twenty-four, in 1133, he became a monk under the first abbot, William, a disciple of S. Bernard. In spite of the delicacy of his body he set himself cheerfully to practise the greatest austerities, and employed much of his time in prayer and reading. His heart turned with great ardour to the love of God, and this made him feel all his mortifications sweet and light. "Thy yoke doth not oppress, but raiseth the soul; thy burden hath wings, not weight," said he. He speaks of divine charity with love, and by his frequent ejaculations on the subject, it seems to have been the sweet consolation of his soul. "May thy voice (says he) sound in my ears, O Good Jesus, that my heart may learn how to love thee, that my mind may love thee, that the interior powers, the bowels of my soul, and very marrow of my heart may love thee, and that my affections may embrace thee, my only true good, my sweet and delightful joy! O my God! He who loves thee possesses thee; and he possesses thee in proportion as he loves, because thou art love itself. This is that abundance with which thy beloved are inebriated, dissolved to themselves, that they may live into thee, by loving thee." He had been much delighted in his youth with reading Cicero; but after his conversion found that author, and all other reading, tedious and bitter, which was not sweetened with the honey of the holy name of Jesus, and seasoned with the word of God, as he says in the preface to his book *On Spiritual Friendship*. He was much edified with the very looks of a holy monk, called Simon, who had despised high birth, an ample fortune, and all the advantages of mind and body, to serve God in that penitential state. This monk went and came as one deaf and dumb, always recollected in God; and was such a lover of silence, that he would scarce speak a few words to the prior on necessary occasions. His silence however was sweet, agreeable, and full of edification. Our Saint says of him, "The very sight of his humility stifled my pride, and made me blush at the want of mortification in my looks." This holy monk, having served God eight years in perfect fidelity, died in 1142, in wonderful peace, repeating with his last breath, "I will sing eternally, O Lord, thy mercy, thy mercy, thy mercy!"

S. Aelred, much against his inclination, was made abbot of a new monastery of his order, founded by William, Earl of Lincoln, at Revesby, in Lincolnshire, in 1142, and after, in 1143, of Rievaulx, where he governed three hundred monks. Describing their life, he says that they drank nothing but water, ate little, laboured hard, slept little, and on hard boards; never spoke, except to their superiors on necessary occasions; and loved prayer.

S. GODRICK, H.

(A.D. 1170.)

[Anglican and Monastic Martyrologies, Molanus and the Bollandists. Authorities :—A life by Reginald of Durham, written at the request of S. Ailred of Rievaulx, whilst S. Godrick was still alive, and presented to S. Ailred. It must have been written before 1166, the year in which S. Ailred died. This life, from an early copy in the British Museum, has been published by the Surtees Society, Durham, 1845. Another life, also by a contemporary, Galfred monk of Finchale, derived mostly from Reginald. The following life is condensed from the charming sketch of S. Godrick by Mr. C. Kingsley in "The Hermits."]

In a loop of the river Wear, near Durham, there settled in the days of Bishop Flambard, between 1099 and 1128, a man whose parentage and history was for many years unknown to the good folks of the neighbourhood. He had come, it seems, from a hermitage in Eskdale, in the parish of Whitby, whence he had been driven by the Percys, lords of the soil. He had gone to Durham, become the doorkeeper of S. Giles's Church, and gradually learnt by heart (he was no scholar) the whole Psalter. Then he had gone to S. Mary's Church, where, as was the fashion of the times, there was a children's school; and, listening to the little ones at their lessons, picked up such hymns and prayers as he thought would suffice his spiritual wants. And then, by leave of the bishop, he had gone away into the woods, and devoted himself to the solitary life in Finchale.

Buried in the woods and crags of the "Royal Park," as it was then called, which swarmed with every kind of game, there was a little flat meadow, rough with sweet-gale and bramble and willow, beside a teeming salmon-pool. Great wolves haunted the woods, but Godrick cared nought for them; and the shingles swarmed with snakes,—probably only the harmless collared snakes of wet meadows, but reputed, as all snakes are by the vulgar, venomous; but he did not object to become "the companion of serpents and poisonous asps." He handled them, caressed them, let them lie by the fire in swarms on winter nights, in the little cave which he had hollowed in the ground and thatched with turf. Men told soon how the snakes obeyed him; how two especially huge ones used to lie twined about his legs; till after many years, annoyed by their importunity, he turned them all gently out of doors, with solemn adjurations never to return, and they, of course, obeyed.

His austerities knew no bounds. He lived on roots and berries, flowers and leaves; and when the good folk found him out, and put gifts of food near his cell, he carried them up to the crags above, and, offering them solemnly up to the God who feeds the ravens when they call on him, left them there for the wild birds. He watched, fasted, and scourged himself, and wore always a hair shirt and an iron cuirass. He sat, night after night, even in mid-winter, in the cold Wear, the waters of which had hollowed out a rock near by into a natural bath, and afterwards in a barrel sunk in the floor of a little chapel of wattle, which he built and dedicated to the blessed Virgin

Mary. He tilled a scrap of ground, and ate the grain from it, mingled with ashes. He kept his food till it was decayed before he tasted it; and led a life, the records of which fill the reader with astonishment, not only at the man's iron strength of will, but at the iron strength of the constitution which could support such hardships, in such a climate, for a single year.

A strong and healthy man must Godrick have been, to judge from the accounts (there are two, both written by eye-witnesses) of his personal appearance—a man of great breadth of chest and strength of arm; black-haired, hook-nosed, deep-browed, with flashing grey eyes; altogether a personable and able man, who might have done much work and made his way in many lands. But what his former life had been he would not tell.

The prologue to the Harleian manuscript (which the learned editor, Mr. Stevenson, believes to be an early edition of Reginald's own composition) confesses that Reginald, compelled by Ailred of Rievaulx, tried in vain for a long while to get the hermit's story from him.

"You wish to write my life?" he said. "Know then that Godrick's life is such as this:—Godrick, at first a gross rustic, an unclean liver, an usurer, a cheat, a perjurer, a flatterer, a wanderer, pilfering and greedy; now a dead flea, a decayed dog, a vile worm; not a hermit, but a hypocrite; not a solitary, but a gad-about in mind; a devourer of alms, dainty over good things, greedy and negligent, lazy and snoring, ambitious and prodigal, one who is not worthy to serve others, and yet every day beats and scolds those who serve him; this, and worse than this, you may write of Godrick." "Then he was silent as one indignant," says Reginald, "and I went off in some confusion," and the grand old man was left to himself and to his God.

The ecclesiastical Boswell dared not mention the subject again to his hero for several years, though he came often from Durham to visit him, and celebrate mass for him in his little chapel. After some years, however, he approached the matter again, and the old man began to answer questions, and Reginald delighted to listen and note down till he had finished, he says, that book of his life and miracles;[1] and after a while brought it to the saint, and falling on his knees, begged him to bless, in the name of God, and for the benefit of the faithful, the deeds of a certain religious man, who had suffered much for God in this life, which he (Reginald) had composed accurately. The old man perceived that he himself was the subject, blessed the book with solemn words, and bade Reginald conceal it till his death, warning him that a time would come when he should suffer rough and bitter things on account of that book, from those who envied him. That prophecy, says Reginald, came to pass; but how, or why, he does not tell.

The story which Godrick told was wild and beautiful; and though we must not depend too much on the accuracy of the old man's recollections, or on the honesty of Reginald's report, who would naturally omit all incidents which were made against his hero's perfection, it is worth listening to, as a vivid sketch of the doings of a real human being, in that misty distance of the Early Middle Age.

He was born, he said, at Walpole, in Norfolk, on the old Roman sea-bank, between the Wash and the deep Fens. His father's name was Ædlward; his mother's, Ædwen—"the Keeper of Blessedness," and "the Friend of Blessedness," as Reginald translates them—poor and

[1] The earlier one; that of the Harleian MSS., which (Mr. Stevenson thinks) was twice afterwards expanded and decorated by him.

pious folk; and, being a sharp boy, he did not take to field-work, but preferred wandering the Fens as a pedlar, first round the villages, then, as he grew older, to castles and to towns, buying and selling—what, Reginald does not tell us: but we should be glad to know.

One day he had a great deliverance. Wandering along the great tide-flats near Spalding and the old Well-stream, in search of waifs and strays, of wreck or eatables, he saw three porpoises stranded far out upon the banks. Two were alive, and the boy took pity on them (so he said) and let them be: but one was dead, and off it (in those days poor folk ate anything) he cut as much flesh and blubber as he could carry, and toiled back towards the high-tide mark. But whether he lost his way among the banks, or whether he delayed too long, the tide came in on him up to his knees, his waist, his chin, and at last, at times, over his head. The boy made the sign of the cross, and struggled on valiantly a full mile through the sea, like a brave lad, never loosening his hold of the precious porpoise-meat till he reached the shore at the very spot from which he had set out.

As he grew, his pedlar journeys became longer. Repeating to himself, as he walked, the Creed and the Lord's Prayer—his only lore—he walked for four years through Lindsey; then went to S. Andrew's, in Scotland; after that, for the first time, to Rome. Then the love of a wandering sea life came on him, and he sailed with his wares round the east coasts; not merely as a pedlar, but as a sailor himself, he went to Denmark and to Flanders, buying and selling, till he owned (in what port we are not told, but probably in Lynn or Wisbeach) half one merchant ship, and the quarter of another. A crafty steersman he was, a wise weather-prophet, a shipman stout in body and in heart.

But gradually there grew on the sturdy merchantman the thought that there was something more to be done in the world than making money. He became a pious man. He worshipped at S. Cuthbert's hermitage at Farne, and there, he said afterwards, he longed for the first time for the rest and solitude of the hermitage. He had been sixteen years a seaman now, with a seaman's temptations—it may be (as he told Reginald plainly) with some of a seaman's vices. He may have done things which lay heavy on his conscience. But it was getting time to think about his soul. He took the cross, and went off to Jerusalem, as many a man did then, under difficulties incredible, dying, too of ten, on the way. But Godrick not only got safe thither, but went out of his way home by Spain to visit the sanctuary of S. James of Compostella.

Then he appears as steward to a rich man in the Fens, whose sons and young retainers, after the lawless fashion of those Anglo-Norman times, rode out into the country round to steal the peasants' sheep and cattle, skin them on the spot, and pass them off to the master of the house as venison taken in hunting. They ate and drank, roystered and rioted, like most other young Normans; and vexed the staid soul of Godrick, whose nose told him plainly enough, whenever he entered the kitchen, that what was roasting had never come off a deer. In vain he protested and warned them, getting only insults for his pains. At last he told his lord. The lord, as was to be expected, cared nought about the matter. Let the lads rob the English villains: for what other end had their grandfathers conquered the land? Godrick punished himself, as he could not punish them, for the unwilling share which he had had in the wrong. It may be that he, too, had eaten of that stolen food. So away he went into France, and down the Rhone, on pilgrimage to the hermitage of

S. Giles, the patron saint of the wild deer; and then on to Rome a second time, and back to his poor parents in the Fens.

And now follows a strange and beautiful story. All love of seafaring and merchandise had left the deep-hearted sailor. The heavenly and the eternal, the salvation of his sinful soul, had become all in all to him; and yet he could not rest in the little dreary village on the Roman bank. He would go on pilgrimage again. Then his mother would go likewise, and see S. Peter's church, and the pope, and all the wonders of Rome. So off they set on foot; and when they came to ford or ditch, Godrick carried his mother on his back, until they came to London town. And there Ædwen took off her shoes, and vowed out of devotion to the holy apostles Peter and Paul to walk barefoot to Rome and barefoot back again.

Now just as they went out of London, on the Dover road, there met them in the way the loveliest maiden they had ever seen, who asked to bear them company in their pilgrimage. And when they agreed, she walked with them, sat with them, and talked with them with superhuman courtesy and grace; and when they turned into an inn, she ministered to them herself, and washed and kissed their feet, and then lay down with them to sleep, after the simple fashion of those days. But a holy awe of her, as of some Saint or Angel, fell on the wild seafarer; and he never, so he used to aver, thought of her for a moment save as a sister. Never did either ask the other who they were, and whence they came; and Godrick reported (but this was long after the event) that no one of the company of pilgrims could see that fair maid, save he and his mother alone. So they came safe from Rome, and back to London town; and when they were at the place outside Southwark, where the fair maid had met them first, she asked permission to leave them, for she "must go to her own land, where she had a tabernacle of rest, and dwelt in the house of her God." And then, bidding them bless God, who had brought them safe over the Alps and across the sea, and all along that weary road, she went on her way, and they saw her no more

Then with this fair mysterious face clinging to his memory, and it may be never leaving it, Godrick took his mother safe home, and delivered her to his father, and bade them both after awhile farewell, and wandered across England to Penrith, and hung about the churches there, till some kinsmen of his recognised him, and gave him a psalter (he must have taught himself to read upon his travels), which he learnt by heart. Then, wandering ever in search of solitude, he went into the woods and found a cave, and passed his time therein in prayer, living on green herbs and wild honey, acorns and crabs; and when he went about to gather food, he fell down on his knees every few yards and said a prayer, and rose and went on.

After awhile he wandered on again, until at Wolsingham, in Durham, he met with another holy hermit, who had been a monk at Durham, living in a cave in forests in which no man dare dwell, so did they swam with packs of wolves; and there the two good men dwelt together till the old hermit fell sick, and was like to die. Godrick nursed him, and sat by him, to watch for his last breath. For the same longing had come over him which came over Marguerite d'Angoulême when she sat by the dying bed of her favourite maid of honour—to see if the spirit, when it left the body, were visible, and what kind of thing it was: whether, for instance, it was really like the little naked babe which is seen in mediæval illuminations flying out of the mouths of dying men. But, worn out with watching, Godrick could not keep from sleep. All but desparing of his desire, he turned to the dying man, and spoke, says Reginald, some such words as these:—"O spirit! who art diffused in that body in the likeness of God, and art still inside that breast, I adjure thee by the Highest, that thou leave not the prison of this thine habitation while I am overcome by sleep, and know not of it." And so he fell asleep: but when he woke, the old hermit lay motionless and breathless. Poor Godrick wept, called on the dead man, called on God; his simple heart was set on seeing this one thing. And behold, he was consoled in a wondrous fashion. For about the third hour of the day the breath returned. Godrick hung over him, watching his lips. Three heavy sighs he drew, then a shudder, another sigh: and then (so Godrick was believed to have said in after years) he saw the spirit flit.

What it was like, he did not like to say, for the most obvious reason—that he saw nothing, and was an honest man. A monk teased him much to impart to him this great discovery. Godrick answered wisely enough, that "no man could perceive the substance of the spiritual soul."

Another pilgrimage to the Holy Sepulchre did Godrick make before he went to the hermitage in Eskdale, and settled finally at Finchale. And there about the hills of Judæa he found hermits dwelling in rock-caves as they had dwelt since the time of S. Jerome. He washed himself, and his hair shirt and little cross, in the sacred waters of the Jordan, and returned, after incredible suffering, to become the saint of Finchale.

At Finchale S. Godrick died on the octave of the Ascension, May 21st. This fixes the date of his death as 1179, for in that year Easter Day fell on April 5th.

His hermitage became, in due time, a stately priory, with its community of monks, who loved the memory of their holy father Godrick. The place is all ruinate now; the memory of S. Godrick gone; and not one in ten thousand, perhaps, who visit those crumbling walls beside the rushing Wear, has heard of the sailor-saint, and his mother, and that fair maid who tended them on their pilgrimage.

Also published by
Llanerch:

TWO CELTIC SAINTS:
THE LIVES OF NINIAN & KENTIGERN.

THE LIFE OF ST. COLUMBA.

LIVES OF THE SCOTTISH SAINTS

NORTHUMBRIAN CROSSES

SYMBOLISM OF THE CELTIC CROSS

For a complete list,
write to:
LLANERCH ENTERPRISES,
Llanerch, Felinfach,
Lampeter, Dyfed,
Wales, SA48 8PJ.